GW00891464

NO COMMENT

Censorship, secrecy and the Irish Troubles

October 1989
ISBN 1-870798-36-8

ARTICLE 19 is an international human rights organisation established in 1986 to impartially promote and defend the right to freedom of opinion and expression and the right to seek, receive and impart information and ideas through any media and regardless of frontiers. It takes its name from article 19 of the Universal Declaration of Human Rights.

ARTICLE 19 seeks to build an international movement to promote freedom of expression and to defend censorship victims everywhere.

If you wish to support ARTICLE 19, write to: ARTICLE 19, 90 Borough High Street, London SE1 1LL, United Kingdom or to ARTICLE 19, c/o Fund for Free Expression, 485 Fifth Avenue, New York, New York 10017, USA.

ARTICLE 19, The International Centre on Censorship. 90 Borough High Street, London SE1 1LL. United Kingdom. Phone: (01) 403 4822. Fax (01) 403 1943

Table of Contents

iv

FIGHTING CENSORSHIP 91

CONCLUSIONS 97

BIBLIOGRAPHY AND ABBREVIATIONS 103

v

This is the second in a series of censorship reports to be published by ARTICLE 19. The purpose is to provide an impartial, authoritative and readable view on a wide range of themes embracing censorship and the right to freedom of expression and information.

Article 19 of the Universal Declaration of Human Rights

"Everyone has the right to freedom of opinion and expression; this right includes freedom to hold opinions without interference and to seek, receive and impart information and ideas through any media and regardless of frontiers."

"If men are to be precluded from offering their sentiments on a matter which may involve the most serious and alarming consequences that can invite the consideration of mankind, reason is of no use to us; the freedom of speech may be taken away, and dumb and silent we may be led like lambs to the slaughter."

(George Washington 1732 - 1799)

1

1. INTRODUCTION

The publication of this report coincides with the first anniversary of the United Kingdom ban on broadcasting the voices of representatives or supporters of eleven Irish organisations. A similar ban, known as Section 31, already existed in the Irish Republic. These bans represent the most explicit interference with any media since the start of the Irish "Troubles".

The report discusses the bans in the context of the accompanying self-censorship and the many other factors which restrict the flow of information about the conflict. It explores the ways in which the ongoing turmoil in Northern Ireland has led to, or been influenced by, restrictions on information rights and freedoms in the UK and Ireland. In both states a range of information crimes have been defined and public access to opinions and information has been restricted.

The recurrent issues in the report are assaults on the rights of opinion and expression, official and unofficial censorship, self-censorship, restricted access to information, and interference with the communication of knowledge and opinion. Secrecy, privacy, harassment of political activists, intelligence activities and prisoners' rights are matters which are less immediately relevant to the central theme but there is an elementary connection: the relationship between power and information.

What distinguishes democracy from tyranny, and defines the gradations in between, is the degree of freedom with which information, ideas and opinions are free to circulate both vertically - from the people to the authorities by means of election and individual or collective petition, and from the authorities to the people by means of open and responsive government - and horizontally, within institutions and among the people. Anything which restricts that flow, beyond what is

3

absolutely and demonstrably necessary for the defence of society and of individual rights, insults and injures the democratic principle.

Whatever the motivation of censorship, whatever the mechanism, the end result is the same: political debate is impoverished and debased. It is nevertheless important to understand the many facets of the problem. This report takes a qualitative approach: instead of a consecutive listing of, for example, each case of interference in television programmes about Northern Ireland, it considers separately the censorship imposed by legal authority, that which occurs informally by means of political pressure on management, and that which occurs "voluntarily" as broadcasters struggle to work in a regime of intimidation and excessive caution.

The report deals with the information freedom aspects of "special" or anti-terrorist legislation; ordinary law and executive discretion; broadcasting law; "informal" and unofficial forms of censorship; official secrecy and access to information; the interception and surveillance of communications; self-censorship, and the struggle against censorship and secrecy.

Each section is illustrated with examples and summaries of legislation and debates, rather than exhaustive cataloguing of incidents and verbatim quotation. The main text is preceded by this introduction, which includes a resumé of the background to the Troubles, and is followed by a bibliography and list of contacts. [1]

It is not the contention of this report that the special circumstances of Northern Ireland can be ignored in any assessment of the protection of human rights in general or in the case of freedom of expression in particular. There is a serious internal conflict in Northern Ireland. Communal antagonism and the violence and political instability which it sustains provide a constant, demanding challenge for the

4

[1] The report is not concerned with obscenity laws, access to medical records or any other information issue with no direct bearing on the conflict; that is not to say that book censorship in the Republic of Ireland, for example, is irrelevant to a consideration of Unionist perceptions of the Republic.

British and Irish authorities and for the democratic principles to which the peoples and the governments of the two states are committed.

In the case of the freedom of information, freedom of the press and freedom of opinion and expression, the rights which ARTICLE 19 is concerned to defend, the prolonged Northern Ireland crisis has not provoked systematic and total state censorship akin to the controls assumed to be justified in time of war (an assumption that ARTICLE 19 would challenge in any event). Freedom of expression has not been curtailed so dramatically. Rather the report argues this freedom has become a casualty by degrees. It has been the cumulative effects of many often ill-considered measures, pressures and exigencies resulting from the conflict which have seriously eroded that freedom.

In its analyses of the many facets of censorship and secrecy that have developed over Northern Ireland, the report makes clear that it is in Britain and Ireland as a whole, not just Northern Ireland, that freedom of expression has been diminished. This is not only a matter of regret and concern to be accepted as a cost of the conflict; it may even be that, far from assisting in the pacification of the conflict, censorship has prolonged the agony by stifling debate and lending weight to the portrayal of the established government as oppressive, insensitive and indifferent.

Since 1969, some 2,750 people have been killed in Northern Ireland; that scales up to 100,000 deaths in Great Britain, or 415,000 in the United States. The cost in security measures and compensation is measured in thousands of millions of pounds. Those statistics could usefully be carried as a footnote on every page of this report, in that they contain both the defence offered for the erosion of civil liberties in the name of anti- terrorism, and the primary evidence that that strategy has not of itself provided the solution. The killing goes on - some fifty deaths in the first nine months of 1989 - and there is no sign of any end to it.

Background to The Troubles

The central issue is the position of Northern Ireland (widely, but inaccurately, referred to as Ulster), which has since 1921 been a province of the United Kingdom, and was self-governing in most matters from then until 1972 (when direct rule from London was imposed).

The majority of the local population favours the union with Great Britain but the minority aspires to unity with the Irish Republic. Each side feels that the other's aspiration threatens its cultural traditions, rights and identity.

This conflict of interests has created a political discourse which divides the population (of about 1,500,000) according to their acceptance of, or opposition to, the position of the province within the UK. For historical reasons those allegiances correlate very closely with religious affiliations. Social and economic issues, although not excluded from political debate, tend to be addressed in the context of what benefits the particular political/religious community represented by the speaker.

The political parties

Those who defend the status quo, or seek the restoration of the pre-1972 provincial parliament and government at Stormont, are the mainly-Protestant Unionists or Loyalists; their political parties are the Ulster Unionist Party (UUP) and the Democratic Unionist Party (DUP).

Those who seek to establish a united Ireland are the mainly-Catholic Nationalists; most have only a long-term aspiration for unification, and support the Social Democratic and Labour Party (SDLP). A part of the Nationalist community views the struggle for unification as paramount, and as justifying the use of violence; this Republican section votes mainly for Sinn Féin.

There are other political parties but the four mentioned above account for over 80 per cent of the electorate. All four are currently legal, although Sinn Féin, which is the political counterpart of the Irish Republican Army (IRA), has been banned in the past.

The paramilitaries

The principle combatants are the Irish Republican Army (IRA) and other Republican paramilitaries, Loyalist paramilitaries such as the United Defence Association (UDA) and the Ulster Volunteer Force (UVF). The "Provisional" IRA broke away in 1970 from the now-extinct "Official" IRA (which later also gave rise to the Irish National Liberation Army, or INLA). The "Provos" seek British withdrawal and the establishment, or re-establishment, of a republic of all Ireland. To that end the IRA kills soldiers, policemen, prison officers, "establishment" figures such as judges, those regarded as collaborators, spies or informers, dissident Republicans, Loyalist activists, and not a few innocent bystanders. It also destroys commercial premises.

The UDA and UVF seek to maintain the union with Britain by suppressing the Republican insurgency. To date their main tactic has been the random murder of Catholic civilians, although some more selective assassinations have been carried out. The UDA has organised large-scale marches, rallies and street barricades, and has shared platforms with leading Unionist politicians; it is the only paramilitary group not banned by law, perhaps because of its practice of ascribing its murders to the fictional "Ulster Freedom Fighters". (The UVF, the IRA and other private armies have also used fictional cover groups for sectarian killings.)

7

The security forces

The principle security force is the 13,000-strong Royal Ulster Constabulary (RUC, and RUC Reserve). It is permanently armed with several specialist anti-terrorist units, but is otherwise organised on similar lines to most British constabularies, with an appointed Police Authority. Although security policy has at times given a stronger role to the regular British Army, the current strategy emphasises the primacy of the police and has the Army and the locally-recruited Ulster Defence Regiment (UDR) in a support role. The three main UK intelligence agencies (the internal service, popularly known as MI5; the foreign service, MI6; and the signals intelligence organisation, GCHQ) all take a very active interest in Irish affairs. There is further input from military intelligence and special forces such as the SAS, and co-operation with the relevant agencies of the Irish State (including the Garda Special Branch and military intelligence).

Most of the non-violent, constitutional, political debate about Northern Ireland takes place within its borders; there is little public interest in it either in Britain or in the rest of Ireland, and neither national government could honestly describe it as their most urgent priority. Likewise, most of the violence takes place within the North. Occasionally the Troubles spill over into the Republic (Loyalist bombings, Republican bank raids), or into Britain and against British targets in continental Europe (Republican bombings and shootings).

Information rights: the legal context

What are the domestic and international legal frameworks under which information rights (that is, freedom of opinion and expression, and free access to information and ideas) are regulated in the three territories most closely affected by the Northern Ireland conflict?

The UK and Ireland are bound by the 1948 Universal Declaration of Human Rights, which is widely accepted as having the status of general principles of international law. Article 19 of the Declaration (from which the organisation ARTICLE 19 takes its name and mandate) proclaims:

Everyone has the right to freedom of opinion and expression; this right includes freedom to hold opinions without interference and to seek, receive and impart information and ideas through any media and regardless of frontiers.

Other law common to both states restricts the right to make statements which might obstruct the course of justice. This law of "contempt" has only rarely been invoked in ways which could be regarded as censorship in relation to the Troubles: the

British government's attempt to invoke it to silence the media before the 1988 Gibraltar affair inquest was unsuccessful (See below).

The United Kingdom

In 1976 the UK ratified the International Covenant on Civil and Political Rights (ICCPR), article 19 of which expresses the right to information in terms similar to those of the Universal Declaration:

> *1. Everyone shall have the right to hold opinions without interference.*
>
> *2. Everyone shall have the right to freedom of expression; this right shall include freedom to seek, receive and impart information and ideas of all kinds, regardless of frontiers, either orally, in writing or in print, in the form of art, or through any other media of his choice.*

The Covenant then stresses that the rights concerning expression are not unconditional:

> *3. The exercise of the rights ... carries with it special duties and responsibilities. It may therefore be subject to certain restrictions, but these shall only be such as are provided by law and are necessary: (a) for respect of the rights or reputations of others; (b) for the protection of national security or of public order, or of public health and morals.*

The Covenant permits a state to derogate from certain rights in a national emergency including freedom of expression. While the UK government did derogate from certain rights in relation to Northern Ireland until 1984, it did not derogate from article 19.

The UK is one of 23 parties to the Council of Europe Convention for the Protection of Human Rights and

9

Fundamental Freedoms (the European Convention on Human Rights), and is thus bound by its provisions on freedom of expression although they have not been incorporated into any domestic statute. This is a serious anomaly in that some principles of European human rights law carry little weight in English courts, so that litigants can incur the inconvenience, expense and delay of appealing to Europe.

Article 10 of the European Convention states:

> *1. Everyone has the right to freedom of expression. This right shall include freedom to hold opinions and to receive and impart information and ideas without interference by public authority and regardless of frontiers. This article shall not prevent states from requiring the licensing of broadcasting, television or cinema enterprises.*

The third sentence is relevant to the broadcasting ban issue, since authority to license implies the power to impose conditions for operation. The article continues:

> *2. The exercise of this freedom, since it carries with it duties and responsibilities, may be subject to such formalities, conditions, restrictions or penalties as are prescribed by law and are necessary in a democratic society, in the interests of national security, territorial integrity or public safety, for the prevention of disorder or crime, for the protection of the reputation or rights of others, for preventing the disclosure of information received in confidence, or for maintaining the authority and impartiality of the judiciary.*

Responsibility for enforcing the Convention rests (after the exhaustion of the domestic procedures) with the European Commission of Human Rights, and subsequently with either the European Court of Human Rights or the Committee of Ministers of the Council of Europe.

As with the UN Covenant of 1976 above, a government may derogate from certain rights in the European Convention in a national emergency. The UK has entered a derogation in the past but not as regards Article 10.

The UK has no written constitution, nor is there a Bill of Rights or similar fundamental law guaranteeing freedom of information. Indeed the major piece of law in this area is concerned entirely with official secrecy and the prevention of access to information. British law imposes a number of other restrictions on the freedom of information, those which have a bearing on the Northern Ireland situation being referred to in the following chapters. Other legislation includes the Race Relations Act 1976, which outlaws incitement to racial hatred and discrimination.

Northern Ireland

As part of the UK, Northern Ireland is bound by treaty to observe the European Convention and the International Covenant. Legislation exists, but is rarely used, to punish incitement to hatred on religious grounds, or to violence. There is no specific protection in Northern Ireland law for freedom of information. Political representatives of both communities support the campaign for a local Bill of Rights, which would presumably contain provisions on the right to information.

11

The Republic of Ireland

The Irish Republic (formally called Ireland, or Eire) is not one of the 87 countries which have so far ratified the ICCPR, but it is a party to the European Convention and has undertaken to comply with judgments of the European Court of Human Rights.

The Constitution of 1937 offers a cautious guarantee of freedom of expression, assembly and association, including the freedom to oppose government policy. Under Article 40 "organs of public opinion" may not be permitted to undermine "public order or morality or the authority of the State" and the publication of "seditious matter" may be punished. "Fidelity to the Nation and loyalty to the State" are the "fundamental political duties of all citizens", but that ostensibly dangerous clause has had no practical effect: no-one has been charged with treason for over 50 years.

The Republic's extensive restrictions on access by "subversives" to the airwaves, introduced in 1976, are posited in terms of the constitutional duty to protect the state's authority, but no attempt has been made to apply it outside the state-licensed broadcasting sector. Legislation and administrative practice affecting freedom of expression and information are considered in detail below. Ireland is almost alone in Europe in not having enacted legislation outlawing racial discrimination, incitement or propaganda.

2. SPECIAL LEGISLATION

The legal aspects of secrecy, censorship and freedom of opinion, expression and information arise in two ways. Firstly, there are criminal laws of a "temporary", "emergency" or exceptional nature, brought in to deal with political subversion and violence; secondly, there are restrictive measures under ordinary law and administrative practice.

There are at present three main pieces of special legislation in force largely as a result of the violence in Northern Ireland. In the province there is the Emergency Provisions Act (EPA); there and in the rest of the UK there is the Prevention of Terrorism Act (PTA); and in the Irish Republic there is the Offences Against the State Act (OASA). Each statute grants certain additional powers of arrest and detention, and defines certain categories of (politically-motivated) offences. This report is concerned only with the provisions concerning information, and the ways in which they have been enforced.

Emergency Provisions Act

13

The information-based crimes defined by Section 21 of the 1978 EPA, as amended by Section 9 of the 1987 EPA, include soliciting or inviting support for an organisation proscribed in Schedule 2 of the Act (the IRA and associated organisations, the UFF, the UVF and so on). It is also illegal to arrange a meeting in support of a banned group.

Space precludes a proper discussion here of whether the power to proscribe organisations is itself an infringement of freedom of expression; it is more clearly an infringement of freedom of association. It has to date been used only against paramilitary organisations rather than political parties. If it should be used against Sinn Féin or any other party, and there are many who call for such action, this would raise serious issues of freedom of expression.

In the "support" clauses the substance of the crime is the expression, or facilitating of the expression, of a political opinion insofar as it invites or solicits support for an illegal organisation. It is not a requirement that anyone is injured or offended; it is not even a requirement that the expression gives rise, or would or might give rise, to a breach of the peace or to some criminal act. While that law stands, anyone who, for example, expresses support for the IRA in a private meeting may be liable to be sent to prison for 10 years and to be fined an unlimited amount. No prosecutions have been brought under this part of the EPA.

The EPA is subject to regular official monitoring and annual renewal by Parliament, but that tends to be a perfunctory affair unless amendments are proposed. Some clauses are altered or deleted, but the essence remains, including the power to reinstate internment (Section 12), which has been used against political dissidents when there is no sustainable evidence of any criminal offence; to that extent it can be regarded as a censorship measure. No one, however, has been detained without trial in Northern Ireland since 1975.

Prevention of Terrorism Act

The PTA was rushed through the UK Parliament, as the Prevention of Terrorism (Temporary Provisions) Act 1974, in the aftermath of IRA bombings in Britain. The Act was revised in 1976 and renewed annually until 1984, when its application was extended to non- Irish terrorism. A new non-temporary version of the PTA was enacted in 1989.

Among provisions which affect freedom of opinion and expression are the Home Secretary's power to prohibit people, including British subjects from Northern Ireland, from remaining in or entering Britain. There are also, in Sections 10 and 14, provisions similar to those of the EPA in respect of membership of, or inviting support for, proscribed organisations, the list of which corresponds partly to that under the EPA.

There have been many allegations that the PTA powers of arrest and detention are routinely used to harass and intimidate Irish activists in Britain, and to trawl for political

14

intelligence, rather than to prevent or investigate acts of terrorism; only a very small percentage of those held under the PTA are subsequently convicted of offences under the Act. Numerous well-publicised cases have involved the use of "port powers" of examination, and the powers of longer detention or expulsion, against political or trade union activists travelling between Ireland and Britain.

The PTA, and indeed the other two laws referred to, also define crimes wherein the offence is the refusal to impart information. It is, for example, a crime to refuse to disclose identity and movements to officers questioning one under the Act. Under Section 11 it is also a crime to withhold information concerning acts of terrorism, or which might help apprehend terrorists. This was at first interpreted in broadcasting circles as making it impossible to interview terrorists; five years passed before the BBC broke the supposed ban, and narrowly avoided prosecution, when it interviewed an INLA representative (see Chapter 6).

The PTA 1989 (Clause 17, Schedule 7) infringes on the privacy of the individual by giving the police enormous powers of access to what were formerly regarded as privileged documents, for example bank and medical records and solicitors' files; they need only say that they want the documents in connection with a "terrorist investigation". The legislation, despite its dangers, has had support because of its objective, the uncovering of paramilitary funds and racketeering.

15

Exclusion and deportation

The PTA power to exclude an individual from all or part of the UK was backed up by new clauses in the 1988 Immigration Act which provided a streamlined, non-judicial, deportation procedure. Previous use of UK immigration law for clearly political ends - the Agee and Hosenball affair, for example - suggests that NI-related expulsions may now be carried out under the PTA or the Immigration Act depending on whether the individuals affected would normally have the right of abode (mainly British, Irish and other EC citizens). In at least one case (Vogel, 1989) a Belfast court has imposed exclusion as a bail condition.

Expulsion has been used as a means of censorship. Martin Galvin, publicity director of the IRA's US support group Noraid, was deported in 1984 for expressing approval of an IRA killing. The expulsion enabled Galvin to present himself in the United States as something of a martyr.

The porosity of the long Irish border allowed him to return in August 1984 via the Republic; because of the exclusion order, police attempted to arrest him as he addressed a rally, and in the melée the RUC shot a man dead with a plastic bullet in front of television cameras. In July-August 1989 Sinn Féinn hosted another visit by Galvin, at the end of which he was publicly arrested and flown to Washington DC by the RAF. Many newspapers carried pictures of his arrest; others, such as *The Guardian*, declined to do so on the grounds that it was a staged "photo-opportunity", but reported the facts.

Exclusion orders had previously been used in 1982 to prevent three elected SF members of the Northern Ireland Assembly from entering Great Britain where they had been invited to address the Greater London Council (both elected bodies have since been dissolved). One, Gerry Adams, has since been elected to the Westminster Parliament and regained his freedom of movement, but the other two - including SF's Director of Publicity, Danny Morrison - remain banned.

It would require a lengthy examination of secret information to establish whether exclusion orders have been made on political, as opposed to security, grounds. However it is to be presumed that orders would not be made at all if there was enough evidence to secure a criminal conviction and imprisonment; Enoch Powell, a former UUP MP, denounced them in February 1989 as a form of internal exile. The executive procedures under which the orders are made are, prima facie, a breach of natural justice and of the due process provisions of Article 6 of the European Convention: reasons are not given and there is no judicial appeal. At present about 104 PTA exclusion orders are in force.

Offences Against the State Act

The 1939 Offences Against the State Act empowered the Irish government to outlaw subversive organisations and publications. A "Suppression Order" was used in 1939 to ban the IRA, which remains illegal in the Republic. Several other paramilitary groups have been banned, including the UDA, although it remains legal in the North.

The power under Section 10 to ban or seize publications has fallen into disuse; *An Phoblacht/ Republican News*, the pro-IRA newspaper, is sold openly in the Republic, as it is in the North and Britain. (Paper sellers are occasionally harassed or moved on by police under ordinary powers, e.g. for causing an obstruction.) However it remains in the statute, as does a clause making it illegal to print in any newspaper or periodical a statement from, or purportedly from, a banned organisation; in practice newspapers are not prosecuted for quoting from IRA communiques, but there is a self-censorship effect. Printed matter (with a few exceptions) must carry the name and address of the publisher, a provision inherited from old English anti-pamphlet laws.

One of the most controversial uses of the Act in recent times led to a five year prison sentence, passed in 1988, on a Cork man, Don O'Leary, for possession of a pro-IRA poster which had been on open sale for some years. The OASA defines as a "seditious document" any paper, photograph, videotape or whatever which advances the claim of a group, in this case the IRA, to act as an alternative government, parliament or army, and possession is a criminal offence. "Incriminating documents" are those which are issued or used by a banned organisation and possession of one is enough to convict a person of membership of that organisation (as is the unsupported belief of a senior Garda that the person is a member). Refusal to surrender seditious or incriminating documents is also a crime.

The OASA has many provisions directly comparable to those of the EPA and the PTA; for example, it is illegal to hold meetings in support of banned organisations. Internment, last used in 1957-62, can be invoked against persons prejudicing peace, order or state security. The OASA also gives the Garda wide powers of arrest and detention, which, as in the UK, are used extensively against political activists with only a small percentage ultimately being charged under the Act. Unlike the EPA and the PTA there is no regular review of the legislation, which is permanent.

Other special powers

Between 1870 and 1986 some 70 pieces of "emergency" legislation were applied in all or part of Ireland, and current restrictions on freedom of information and expression are not confined to those in the EPA, PTA and OASA.

The Public Order (NI) Order 1987 (Article 9) defines an offence of using threatening, abusive or insulting words likely to arouse hatred or fear. There are similar, but more explicitly anti-sectarian, provisions in the Incitement to Hatred Act, and some particularly outspoken individuals have been successfully prosecuted. The Republic has no incitement law at present but one has been proposed.

It can be argued that restrictions on freedom of expression should only be introduced and/or enforced where there is an actual or threatened breach of the peace as a direct and intended consequence of the utterance or publication concerned. In the Northern Ireland context, intemperate language is a perpetual and popular feature of political discourse; in most cases it is simple hyperbole, rabble-rousing oratory, with no serious intent or consequence. Fiery talk is little more than an echo of a chronically violent and intolerant political climate, and the causes of that violence and intolerance should be addressed more earnestly than its verbal reflection.

A related issue is the exercise of powers to ban or restrict marches and rallies: unless public order is clearly at risk, it can be seen as an interference with the right of expression. There are allegations from both NI communities of bias in making the decisions; Loyalists maintain that they ought to be free to demonstrate their allegiance in any part of the realm, but Nationalists denounce as provocations any Loyalist parades allowed through mainly Catholic areas (notably in Keady, and Garvaghy Road in Portadown) and say that they are denied

18

similar opportunities (for example, the Drumcree Faith and Justice Group was prohibited in July 1989 from parading in central Portadown). However, prohibitions and restrictions affect only a few of almost 2,000 Loyalist and 200 Nationalist parades held each year (1988 figures).

Defunct legislation

Several old pieces of legislation which imposed even more severe limitations on freedom of expression have been replaced, abolished or have fallen into disuse.

Perhaps the most notorious was the Special Powers Act, which gave the former Stormont authorities proscriptive powers similar to those under the EPA. They were used in 1967 in an attempt to stifle the political and propaganda activity of what was then an entirely non-violent Republican movement: the Republican Clubs, later to evolve into the Workers' Party, were banned, and the House of Lords upheld that banning (*McEldowney v Forde*). It was rescinded in 1973. The ban convinced some in the Nationalist community that the Stormont system was irreformable and that British courts could not be relied upon to protect Nationalists.

The Flags and Emblems Act 1954 allowed the police to prohibit the display in Northern Ireland of the Irish flag, the tricolour, which one-third of the local population regarded as their own national emblem. The Act was repealed in 1987; it is now only an offence to display a flag (union jack or tricolour) where it is likely to lead to a breach of the peace.

19

The Incitement to Disaffection Act 1934 was used in the early 1970s to prosecute a group of pacifists who gave troops leaflets opposing the British presence in Northern Ireland. The case brought considerable criticism on the authorities although a complaint to Strasbourg over the conviction was rejected by the European Commission of Human Rights. There were subsequent prosecutions under the Act in the 1970's but no convictions.

3. BROADCASTING LAW

This chapter is concerned with the legal environment within which the broadcasting systems of the UK and Ireland operate, and restrictions on access to the airwaves: non-legal restrictions, and campaigns against restrictions, are considered separately.

Neither state censors the views of dissident groups in the print media, but both have imposed severe restrictions on radio and television. This is partly because the broadcast media are relatively new and, despite general acceptance of the freedom of the printed press, it was held that official regulation and licensing was required to ensure proper allocation of broadcast frequencies. In that instance regulation may protect freedom of expression, so long as competing views are heard on the licensed stations: whereas newspapers do not interfere with each other's right to be read, two stations broadcasting on the same wavelength can drown each other out. Technological developments have undermined that argument, which in any event did not justify control over the *content* of broadcasts. However, in Britain and Ireland there developed large and centralised bureaucracies to administer the broadcasting systems, by their nature more amenable to government intervention than the myriad autonomous press operations.

Secondly, governments have perceived important differences in the ways in which print and broadcasting address their respective audiences. Broadcasting is seen as more immediate and as having more effect, with information and ideas thrown serially at the audience and with order and pace dictated by the presenter; conversely print allows for contemplation, inviting the reader to ignore or to absorb each item. Earl Ferrers, announcing the 1988 UK ban in the House of Lords [2], took this view: "It is the immediacy of radio and especially of television that does the harm... Second-hand reports in the press do not have the same impact."

It is possible to challenge these assumptions: broadcast media may be seen as more novel than different, so that they ought not to be subject to any different regulation to the print media.

The government also maintained that "those who apologise for terrorism gain a spurious respectability when treated in broadcasts as though they were constitutional politicians"; that begs two questions - had broadcasters ever interviewed "apologists for terrorism" without making it clear which movements those people represented; and would the ban have been unnecessary if interviewers agreed to treat such interviewees more aggressively?

Northern Ireland broadcasting is covered by UK law and practice, with almost all legal television and radio coming under either the British Broadcasting Corporation (BBC) or the Independent Broadcasting Authority (IBA). The Republic of Ireland has one national broadcasting authority, Radio Telefis Eireann (RTE), and a number of independent, mainly local, radio stations.

The United Kingdom

22

The BBC operates under a Licence and Agreement, the current version of which dates from 2nd April 1981. The IBA, however, is regulated by the Broadcasting Act 1981. The regimes under which both operate are similar; specifically, Clause 13(4) of the Licence and Agreement, and Section 29(3) of the Act, recognise that the Home Secretary has extensive power to determine what may and may not be broadcast. The Wireless Telegraphy Act describes broadcasting licences as "subject to such terms, provisions and limitations as the [Home] Secretary ... may think fit", including "the persons by whom the station may be used".

The IBA is shortly to be replaced with separate television and radio authorities, but the government is not expected to relinquish any of its power. There is a separate Cable Authority to regulate the small amount of cable television broadcasting.

The BBC had a monopoly of broadcasting in Northern Ireland until 1959, when Ulster Television (UTV) was established. An independent radio station also operates under the IBA. Until the 1960s broadcasting was aligned with the Unionist establishment; there was minimal coverage of Nationalist culture or politics.[3] The national networks took little interest in the province, and when they did report it, generally filtered coverage through the local management. Both systems extended and developed their coverage over the past 25 years, permitting access for such things as Gaelic sports, and they had come to be regarded by both sections of the NI population as generally impartial and reliable (although BBC NI journalist Barry Cowan has said[4] "the fact that the word *British* is etched in stone over our front door means that one-third of our audience views us with intense suspicion").

It appears that the lessons learned as to how extension of access increases the acceptability and effectiveness of the media have now been unlearned, at least at governmental level.

The 1988 ban

23

On 19th October 1988 the Home Secretary, Douglas Hurd, issued notices to the BBC and the IBA worded as follows (extracts):

> *I hereby request the [BBC and IBA] to refrain at all times from sending any broadcast matter which consists of or includes any words spoken... by a person who... represents*

3> *The Most Contrary Region: the BBC in Northern Ireland 1924 - 1984*, Rex Cathcart.

4> *The Observer* 8.5.88

> *an organisation specified... below, or [when]*
> *the words support or solicit or invite support*
> *for such an organisation.*

The list included five Republican paramilitary groups banned under anti-terrorist legislation - the IRA, its women's and youth wings, the INLA and a long-defunct Republican group called Saor Eire; three illegal Loyalist paramilitary groups - the UVF, the UFF and the Red Hand Commandos; two legal political parties, Sinn Féin and the smaller hard-line Republican Sinn Féin; and one legal Loyalist paramilitary group, the Ulster Defence Association.

Exceptions to the ban allowed voice broadcasting during election campaigns and Westminster parliamentary proceedings. The ban was introduced, as we have seen, under powers already available to the Home Secretary. No parliamentary debate or approval was strictly necessary, although both took place.

Until the ban was introduced few were aware of the extent of the government's control over the broadcast media. The banning power had only been invoked on a handful of occasions in the previous 60 years, most recently in 1964 to prohibit subliminal advertising.

Interpreting the ban

The Home Secretary advised the House of Commons [5] that the Notice applied only to "words spoken by a person who appears or is heard on the programme on which the matter is broadcast where the person speaking the words represents, or purports to represent, one of the organisations specified". (In fact the order also applied to non-representatives who "support or solicit or invite support for" one of the affected organisations.) If the order was disobeyed, he said, "that is a matter for my action against the [BBC and IBA]"; the implication was that the responsible authority would be forced to agree to a severe penalty to avoid the withdrawal or suspension of its licence to broadcast, or the imposition of some

---

5>   *Hansard* 19.10.88

other punishment through a variation of the licence. The measure was thus a form of "prior restraint" censorship, in that it threatened action if anything improper were broadcast, rather than responding to broadcasts which had actually taken place.

The Home Office acknowledged the existence of a substantial loophole in that "the notice permits the showing of a film or still picture of the initiator speaking the words together with a voice-over account of them, in paraphrase or verbatim". Another concession was that elected representatives (meaning in practice the SF MP and councillors) could be interviewed about constituency matters provided that they were not speaking on behalf of a listed organisation; it was left to journalists and management to sort out when a councillor was speaking on his own behalf, and when he was giving the party line.

Mark Bonham-Carter, a former BBC Vice-Chairman, has made the point that "deaf people who can lip-read are exempt from the ban"[6].

On the negative side, the Home Office interpretation was that the notice applied to statements made even in other countries, or in parliaments other than Westminster. Legal advice obtained by Channel 4 TV was that the ban applied retrospectively: it "would cover any material recorded at any time in the past - for example newsreel footage shot before the creation of the Republic of Ireland". There was no requirement that the words spoken be offensive or provocative.

25

Defending the ban

The rationale of the ban was expressed by the Prime Minister shortly after it was imposed: "To beat off your enemy in a war you have to suspend some of your civil liberties for a time"[7]. This suggestion that one "suspends" one's own liberties in order to defeat one's enemy seems to be a recognition of the unpleasant fact that the liberties of ordinary citizens were "suspended" by the ban.

6>   *The Independent* 12.1.88
7>   *The Times* 26.10.88

The Home Secretary dwelt not so much on the alleged usefulness of the ban as on the suggestion that the appearance of the affected individuals had "caused widespread offence". Anticipating a challenge on the basis of international law, he claimed that the ban was "within the bounds of the European Convention... It is not censorship, because it does not deal with or prohibit the reporting of events... Broadly, we are putting broadcasters on the same basis as representatives of the written press". The last is true only in the obvious sense that in the written press the words cannot be heard; there is, however, nothing to stop the papers from allowing anyone full access to their columns. [8]

Almost all the parliamentary and press discussion focused on the IRA and Sinn Féin in relation to television; it was almost as though it was not realised that it applied to radio and to the other groups, and to individuals deemed to be supporting, or soliciting or inviting support, for any of the groups.

Among MPs who welcomed the ban was Ulster Unionist Ken Maginnis, who said it had "considerable merit". Maginnis' party colleague, Rev. William McCrea, was able to proclaim within minutes of the announcement that "the vast majority of people in Northern Ireland, and within the UK" supported the measure. Peter Robinson (DUP) maintained that "it was not [Hurd] who banned Sinn Féin, but, Sinn Féin who (sic) excluded itself by its behaviour". Like some other members, he felt that the ban did not go far enough, and that it should be followed by even more radical measures: he proposed banning SF from local council chambers, and his leader Ian Paisley said, and Harold McCusker (UUP) implied, that SF should be banned. Progressive Unionist Jim Kilfedder said the right to live was more fundamental than the right to free speech.

From the Conservative benches some correctly pointed out that the ban was more liberal than the Irish Republic's Section 31 (see below), while others called for the proscription of Sinn Féin . David Alton (SLD) approved of the ban but his party

---

8> quotations from *Hansard* 19.10.88 or from newspaper coverage in the week after the ban

leader, Paddy Ashdown, opposed it (while calling for SF to be banned from councils) and colleague Robert Maclennan denounced its "sinister consequences".

In the subsequent Commons debate the restrictions were approved by 243 votes to 179.

One of the most extravagant endorsements of the ban came in the upper House from a Labour politician and former Secretary of State for Northern Ireland, Lord (Roy) Mason: "in a democratic society it is defensible to stifle all outlets of those terrorist groups who are bent on undermining the authority of the state and ... smashing our democratic institutions. If we are to cut off the oxygen supply of propaganda - and I welcome this move ... we should also cover the written medium. The present measure is only a half-measure ... We should go the whole hog and stop all propaganda on television, radio and the newspapers."

Lord (Gerry) Fitt, the former SDLP leader, supported what he erroneously termed "this legislation", as did Baroness Stedman (SDP): "we give it a rather low-key approval". Her leader, David Owen, was more certain about the propriety of "restricting the civil rights of the few... to try to protect the many".

Parts of the British press welcomed the ban: "long overdue... sensible and right... [we] wonder why he stopped short of proscribing Sinn Féin" (*Daily Express*); "there should not be one law for the goggle box and another for the ballot box ... Meanwhile half a ban is better than no ban" (*Daily Mail*). *The Sun* appeared to favour the ban; its stablemate *The Times* blamed the ban on terrorism, while the *Sunday Telegraph* blamed the media: the banning "should have been done years ago", but "would have been unnecessary" if the TV companies had exercised "ruthless self-censorship".

The *Daily Star* described it as "a crushing blow... to starve the IRA and other killer gangs of publicity", although commenting on the Rushdie affair three months later, it said "in Britain... we're proud to insist that, whether we disagree or not with what people say, we will defend to the death their right to say it".

27

South African State President P.W. Botha gave it his fulsome backing and the point was made that the UK was no longer in a strong position to criticise the South African censorship measures. [9]

Opposition to the ban

Among Northern Ireland MPs, Seamus Mallon (SDLP) said the damage done was not to the IRA nor the UDA, but to civil liberties. "How many", he asked, "will lay down their guns because they cannot watch Gerry Adams on television?" His colleague Eddie McGrady said "Sinn Féin should be kept fully in the public eye where their hypocrisy can be exposed".

The Labour Party was almost unanimous in its opposition. Former Solicitor General Peter Archer said the ban was "chipping away at the institutions of a free society... because the government find unacceptable the opinions that are likely to be expressed". Tony Benn called it "a massive extension of state control"; Martin Flannery said it was a "measure born of panic [and] a capitulation to... the floggers and hangers"; Ken Livingstone pointed out that the IRA had sustained itself until the 1950s with no access whatever to television. The shadow Home Secretary, Roy Hattersley, regarded the ban as "trivial, worthless and... counter-productive". He pointed out that Gerry Adams MP could appear, if he attended the House, on the BBC's *Today in Parliament* broadcast, but when he left the building it would be impossible to interview him about what he had said.

Merlyn Rees, like Mason a former NI Secretary, said "It is a grave mistake and extremely foolish. The more you see of these people the better; when you try to hide them they seem important." Lord Mishcon asked: "Have we such a poor view of the public that we believe they would accept propaganda in favour of killing innocent women, children and soldiers?" He added that "the appearance of [terrorist spokesmen] - especially with a responsible interviewer - would deflect many from their cause." Lord Harris described the ban as "sledgehammer tactics".

28

9> *The Guardian* 22.10.88; *The Citizen* (Johannesburg) 27.10.88

Some Conservative MPs were deeply troubled by the ban. Cyril Townsend said "we are cold-bloodedly discriminating against a political party in part of our kingdom... this is a measure of censorship"; Tim Rathbone, Andrew Hunter and Hugh Dykes also expressed misgivings.

Among the British press, opposition was expressed across the political spectrum. The *Daily Telegraph* opposed it on four grounds - ineffectiveness, the negative foreign reaction, the precedent set by banning appearances by a legal party, and the preferred alternative strategy of "more effective action by the security forces, and proper consideration of whether Sinn Féin itself should be banned". The *Financial Times* said that "censorship is irrelevant" and the government should tackle the issues of Catholic alienation and Unionist intransigence; the *Daily Mirror* appeared to take a neutral or anti-ban stance. *The Guardian* wondered why "a government which condemns the nanny state" should think the people incapable of seeing through propaganda, and *The Independent* took a similar line. *Today* called the ban "futile", "muddled" and a victory for the IRA, as did *The Observer* and the *Mail on Sunday*, the latter adding that it was "wrong in principle... misguided in practice". *The People* said it was "the tactic of the Eastern Bloc or South Africa, not of a civilised democracy", and *The Sunday Times* had two anti-ban pieces from star columnists. The overall score among the major UK national newspapers was thus six for the ban, ten against; in circulation terms, 9.8 million for, 12.6 million against.

For the BBC, Chairman Marmaduke Hussey and Director General Michael Checkland expressed their unhappiness at "a damaging precedent" which would "make our reporting of Northern Ireland affairs incomplete" [10]. David Nicholas, chief executive of Independent Television News (ITN), said that the ban could damage the fight against terrorism, and Desmond Smith of UTV expressed concern at ambiguous passages in the order. James Hawthorne, former Controller of BBC Northern Ireland, also opposed the ban.

10>   *The Independent* 20.10.88

The NUJ called it "disastrous" [11] pointing out that it negated not only the right to free speech but "a basic civil liberty - the right to have information"[12]. The leader of another media union, the ACTT, said it was "a very dangerous precedent"; the International Federation of Journalists, the Radio Academy and other media organisations also issued protests.

The Irish Times (Dublin) foresaw "a tighter squeeze" when the ban proved unproductive. The communist *Morning Star* (London) said the government was stifling dissent. Among local newspapers, the London *Evening Standard* called the ban "silly and counter-productive". In West Belfast, the *Andersonstown News* accused the government of "disenfranchising the people" of the area.

For one of the three legal organisations targeted by the ban, Sinn Féin president Gerry Adams said: "We will develop alternative means of communication." The UDA, also affected by the ban, failed to come up with a coherent response.

Outside the UK, the *San Francisco Chronicle* [13] echoed statements from the NUJ and from Prof. Kevin Boyle, then Director of ARTICLE 19, by saying "the restrictions are quite similar to those imposed by South Africa... they constitute a fracturing of basic rights". The Iranian news agency IRNA said that the independence of the BBC was "total hypocrisy in view of the ban on Northern Ireland reporting" [14]. *The Wall Street Journal* [15] called it "one of the stupidest moves the Tory government has ever made". "How bizarre", said *The New York Times* [16]; "repressive", said *Prensa Latina* (Cuba) [17].

The subsequent campaign against the ban, and the various attempts to mount a legal challenge, are covered in Chapter 9 (Fighting Censorship).

30

11>   the *Guardian* 1.11.88
12>   *Irish News* (Belfast) 20.10.88
13>   28.10.88
14>   31.10.88
15>   4/5.11.88
16>   3.11.88
17>   22.10.88

The operation of the ban

The ban has now been in force for one year, apart from a suspension in April-May 1989 during elections. It is difficult to quantify the effects strictly attributable to its enforcement, partly because it is unlikely that every instance of its application has become known, but mainly because the extensive self-censorship which existed before its introduction has continued, and has probably had more effect than the strict terms of the ban itself (see Chapter 5).

The ban has been applied conscientiously and completely in respect of official representatives of the affected groups speaking in that capacity. In almost every instance where such a person has been interviewed, summaries or transcripts of what was, said have been broadcast over or instead of the speaker's voice, with television usually showing film of the words being spoken or a still photograph of the speaker. The only exceptions noted (nine in all) fell within the permitted category of elected representatives speaking about constituency matters, as when Gerry Adams MP was interviewed about investment in West Belfast in February 1989, or during the pre-election suspension of the ban in April-May 1989.

The real difficulty has been in policing the "support" clause of the ban. Broadcasters have no way of knowing, short of extracting a confession in advance, that someone who is not a representative of any affected organisation intends to make a statement that will be construed as support, or a solicitation or invitation of support. If they are determined to avoid a breach of the law, they are (a) forced to pre-record and expurgate everything said by anyone whom they suspect might utter, invite or solicit support, and (b) greatly tempted to exercise extensive self-censorship by declining to have such persons on their broadcasts at all.

Programmes affected by the ban

In relation to the main impact of the ban on actuality coverage of Northern Ireland, at least 30 news or other interviews with persons affected by the ban have been broadcast within the ban conditions.

The first phone-in radio broadcast under ban conditions was probably the BBC's *Call Nick Ross* on 25 October 1988; the programme sought to canvass opinion about the ban, but an executive was on hand to cut off anyone whose views could be construed as support for the listed organisations. Two days later a planned live interview on London's LBC radio with members of the United Campaign against Plastic Bullets was dropped in favour of pre-recording it.

Voice-overs of SF speakers were used by the BBC on 19th October (twice), 16th November, 9th and 24th January, 27th January (twice), 28th and 29th January, 16th and 20th March and 14th August. ITV and Channel 4 used voice-overs for SF on 19th October (twice), late October (twice) and 10th November. Subtitles were used for SF by ITV or Channel 4 on 14th November, 13th July, 17th August and 7th September, and by the BBC on 16th November and 9th, 11th and 24th January. Silent film of Republican rallies was shown by the BBC on 26th March, and its coverage of the Galvin arrest on 15th August was also silent. A UDA man was subtitled by the BBC on 27th October. "Health warnings" advising viewers of the ban conditions were given on many of those occasions, and on 11th December, 8th May and 15th August (Channel 4 reports). This listing may not be complete.

The other main intentional effects of the ban relate to historical and archive material. Having received the legal advice referred to above, Channel 4 was forced to re-edit a highly acclaimed 1981 Thames TV series, *The Troubles*, before it could be repeated in 1989, even though the original version had itself been censored in the pre-production stage by the IBA. Many hundreds of other programmes, tapes and films made since the start of sound recording would also have to be censored before re-broadcast.

Channel 4 TV has found itself unable to broadcast a commissioned work from the Derry Film and Video Collective, *Mother Ireland*, which explored the historical and cultural significance of the image of Ireland as woman.

Party political broadcasts

The BBC and IBA are obliged under the Representation of the People Act to give coverage to all election candidates, and both allocate airtime for pre-election advertising by parties. The number and duration of "party politicals", or PPBs, is determined by a formula which permits Sinn Féin several TV and radio slots. The ban is lifted after elections have been called and reimposed directly after polling.

There has been little controversy over PPBs and only a few calls for the exclusion of Sinn Féin from the allocation. However, UUP MP Ken Maginnis has proposed that all other parties desist from using TV during elections to stop Sinn Féin doing so.

The Republic of Ireland

RTE operates two national television channels and three radio channels, and had a near-monopoly in domestic broadcasting until the development in the 1970s of a "pirate" radio sector now legitimised (1989) by the awarding of franchises to commercial and community stations. This developing sector is overseen by an Independent Radio and Television Commission with powers rather more limited than those of the UK IBA. (The broadcasts of the BBC, ITV and Channel 4 are received across most of the Republic.)

RTE is autonomous, but far from independent; its Director-General and management structure are overseen by the RTE Authority, whose members are appointed by the Taoiseach (prime minister). The evidence is that incumbent Taoisigh take a personal interest in these appointments, and give precedence to political associates. The Minister for Posts and Telecommunications has essentially the same licensing powers as the UK Home Secretary, including the power to veto programmes.

The ban on "subversives"

One of the points made by the UK Home Secretary in defence of his own media ban was the prior existence of a similar measure in the Irish Republic; in fact, Mr Hurd told the Commons [18] that the wording his Notice used was largely drawn from the Irish ban's wording. (The Irish government, he said, was not consulted, but was informed in advance of the measure.) In fact, the Irish ban goes rather further than that in the UK, and pre-dates it by many years.

A ministerial directive under the Broadcasting Authority Act can set out "any particular matter or matter of any particular class" which RTE may not transmit. The first such instruction, given in October 1971 by the then Minister Gerry Collins, forbade RTE to transmit anything "that could be calculated to promote the activities of any organisation" engaging in or supporting "the attainment of any particular objective by violent means". That directive was renewed by successive governments.

The reasoning appeared to be that the state, as proprietor or trustee of the public broadcasting system, had the same right as private media owners to intervene in editorial policy to defend its interests, meaning in practice those of the government of the day.

In 1976 an amendment to Section 31 of the Act allowed the imposition of restrictions much more extensive than those enacted in the UK in 1988, in that RTE was prohibited from broadcasting "an interview, **or report of an interview** with a spokesman... for any one or more of the following organisations" (although in practice some reporting has been allowed). The list included Sinn Féin, then as now a legal political party; in fact since 1974 it had been the fourth largest in terms of local council seats in the Republic.

Another censorship power is provided by Section 18 of the Act, under which writer Nell McCafferty was temporarily

34

18> *Hansard* 19.10.88

banned in November 1987 for "incitement to violence"; the Derry-born journalist is no longer used by RTE in programmes connected with Northern Ireland.

Until the 1988 UK ban, the anomaly existed that whereas the national broadcasting system was unable to transmit even a report of an interview with an SF representative, UK channels received in the Republic were able to carry voice interviews.

Attitudes to the ban

Among those who have most vociferously defended the Section 31 ban is academic and journalist Conor Cruise O'Brien, who introduced the 1976 amendment as a minister in a Fine Gael-Labour coalition. He has maintained that the ban, by disabling the political side of the Republican movement, inevitably damages its military side. O'Brien and the then Justice Minister, Paddy Cooney, sought in 1976 to extend the ban to newspapers; a campaign led by the *Irish Press*, and supported by Fianna Fail, killed the plan, and both ministers lost their seats at the next election. Fianna Fail has continued to support Section 31, as do its present coalition partners, the Progressive Democrats, who call it "just and necessary".

The International Federation of Journalists described Section 31 as "indefensible political censorship" [19]. It was attacked on more pragmatic grounds by *The Irish Times*: "There is no more effective way of countering IRA propaganda than by letting it stand on its merits in the market-place."

Journalists who have opposed the ban include Ireland's best-known broadcaster, Gay Byrne, who has said [20] that he would like to be allowed to interview Gerry Adams. Groups campaigning against the ban include the Repeal Section 31 Committee and the recently-formed Media Watch. A legal challenge has also been organised (see Chapter 9).

35

19> *Censoring "the Troubles"*, 1987
20> *Sunday Tribune* 24.9.89

The operation of the ban

In a context which they calculated would not "promote" the IRA, RTE transmitted an interview with the then IRA chief of staff in November 1972; the government dismissed the entire RTE Authority and the reporter involved was imprisoned (see Chapter 4). There were no further challenges to the directive.

The strict terms of the Section 31 prohibition are vigorously enforced, and any appearances on broadcasts by representatives of affected organisations have been accidental - for example, in phone- ins - or, where there is any suspicion that a journalist co-operated, have been punished severely. One RTE reporter, Jenny McGeever, was dismissed after her report on 15th March 1988 of an IRA funeral featured an SF leader addressing mourners and four words spoken on tape by Gerry Adams. The only exception allowed was in 1981, for interviews in a historical series which RTE had co-produced with the BBC. Unlike the UK ban, the Irish one has no exemption for the coverage of elections.

A disquieting feature of Section 31 is the absence of any effective debating or oversight of its operation. The notice is laid before the Dail for annual renewal, but the consensus in its favour among the two main parties - Fianna Fail and Fine Gael - ensures that the requisite majority is recorded with little fuss. Occasionally, questions are asked by backbenchers or members of the smaller parties, but there have never been the seven votes needed to table a blocking motion; there is no requirement for a report, no committee of oversight, no amendment debate and no media interest. The UK ban appears to have borrowed this worst feature of Section 31 in that no provision has been made there for parliamentary scrutiny.

It has been said that Section 31, rather than operating as just another of the many regulations affecting broadcasting, has "taken over" RTE, conditioning its entire editorial ethos and resulting in an overtly cautions line on all news and documentary programmes. With the great capacity of TV to influence popular beliefs and perceptions, Section 31 has even been referred to in psychoanalytic terms as the "national superego", in that its censorious demands, by now internalised

36

at an almost unconscious level, prevent the nation from addressing the crisis from which the ban arose. Self-censorship in radio and television is discussed below in Chapter 8.

Party political broadcasts

In the Republic, as in the UK, airtime is given in the run-up to elections to permit opposing political parties to present their policy positions and manifestoes. Time is allocated to each party fielding more than seven Dail candidates. Sinn Féin has simply been refused PPB airtime by a 1982 ministerial directive under Section 31. The Supreme Court upheld the ban.

4. INFORMAL CENSORSHIP

Censorship does not always consist of laws or bureaucrats telling the media what they cannot print, show or say, or citizens what they cannot read, see or hear. It has many manifestations. Any intentional interference with the free flow of information or ideas is an act of censorship, and many, if not most, such acts take place locally and informally. Examples are the intimidation of journalists, the jeopardising of news cameramen by turning them into police information gatherers, and some uses of contempt-of-court law against the media.

Attacks on journalists

Many journalists have experienced violence or threats in the course of their duties in Northern Ireland. Sometimes this has arisen from antagonism towards a specific journalist or all journalists; sometimes it is to prevent the reporting of a particular event; and sometimes the journalist receives a random blow from bottle or baton. The cumulative effect of such incidents is to make journalists cautious as to how they gather information, and the danger is that some may also become cautious in using the information which they have gathered.

The most serious assault took place in May 1984, when Jim Campbell, Northern editor of the popular tabloid *Sunday World*, was shot and seriously injured by Loyalists. Campbell was eventually well enough to return to work, albeit in offices now protected by security surveillance.

Chris Ryder, *The Sunday Times* correspondent in 1976-77, and Roger Cook, of Central TV in 1988, were threatened respectively by the IRA and the UDA for investigating racketeering. (It would be absurd to suggest that Cook's programme increased support for the racketeers, but under the broadcasting ban, a repeat showing of his encounter with UDA extortionists would require the dubbing or subtitling of their half of the dialogue.)

In 1988, Marty O'Hagan of the *Sunday World* was kidnapped by the IRA and questioned for 12 hours about his sources for a news story. In 1989, a threat was made on the life of the Belfast correspondent of a British national newspaper; he and his family were forced to leave home and he now works from secret and frequently-changed addresses. At least one Belfast journalist is required to carry a gun for his own protection.

In 1989 there were assertions by the RUC, the Secretary of State, the Lord Mayor of Belfast, and sections of the press including *The Sunday Times* and *The Independent*, that visiting news crews had provoked or prolonged riots and behaved intrusively. Similar claims had been made during the hunger strike riots in 1981.

There have been allegations of the harassment of press photographers by the NI security forces. In August 1989 a French photographer, Gilles Favier, alleged he was beaten by the RUC; a German-American freelance, Nick Vogel, who claimed to have been threatened by police after photographing the Favier incident, was arrested for possession of a rifle magazine. Vogel was released on bail with the highly unusual stipulation that he remained outside the province. It was notable in reports of the August events that a number of the pressmen quoted felt the need to insist on anonymity.

At least four press photographers have been hit by rubber or plastic bullets fired by the security forces [21]. The most serious injury occurred to *Daily Mirror* man Cyril Cain in 1981, and press witnesses claimed that he was targeted by the police after unfavourable coverage in the *Mirror*. In June 1988 a claim for damages was made by a photographer alleging assault by two RUC men as he covered an Orange Order parade through a Catholic district. He was allegedly told at gunpoint that he had no right to be there and was allegedly forced to abandon his camera.

21> *The Journalist*, 9.89

Other journalists have been harassed or beaten by paramilitaries or civilians. The *Daily Mirror* correspondent was beaten up in a bar in 1983. A UTV crew was attacked by Loyalists in Limavady in 1985. At an incident in March 1988 in Andersonstown several cameras or films were stolen or destroyed. Later in 1988 Sinn Féin sought to issue its own press cards, but an NUJ protest forced it to back down. A photographer in Derry had his camera seized, but subsequently returned, by the IRA. On many occasions, most recently at a UVF funeral in September 1989, photographers and cameramen have been threatened to prevent coverage of paramilitary gatherings.

Robert Fisk, then of *The Times*, claimed in 1975 that the Army maintained intelligence files on journalists. Several journalists have had evidence that their telephones were tapped, and others have been arrested while working in or coming from Northern Ireland.

Government pressure on the media

Both print and broadcast media are susceptible to informal government pressures, ranging from the discreet lobbying of editors to ministerial harangues against "irresponsible journalism".

In relation to the television networks, a number of such cases have been documented stretching back to the IRA's "border campaign" of the late 1950s. In 1959, NI Prime Minister Lord Brookeborough intervened with the BBC to prevent the screening of an interview with Irish actress Siobhan McKenna and seven planned reports on the North by Alan Whicker. At around the same time, newspaper editors in the Republic were encouraged not to use IRA statements and, where possible, to use euphemisms such as "subversives" rather than name the IRA.

In 1971-72 the BBC was urged by both the UK and NI governments to drop a programme, *The Question of Ulster*, which would confront the issues in the Troubles through a "tribunal" format. As negotiations dragged on, the programme became a *cause célèbre*, and the BBC's insistence on screening it was presented as a demonstration of editorial independence. The Home Secretary, Reginald Maudling, stopped short of using his licence powers to block the programme.

In 1972 the British government sought to prevent the media discussing the 13 killings of civilians by paratroopers on Bloody Sunday, claiming that it could prejudice an official inquiry. Few media challenged the ban, even Thames TV, which showed interviews with serving or former British soldiers, refrained from broadcasting any film of civilian witnesses. In 1974 the NI Secretary tried to prevent the BBC showing a film called *Children in Crossfire*: the Controller of BBC NI had substantial changes made, delayed it twice and inserted a one-minute preface setting out government policy.

In 1976 the BBC destroyed a film on SAS training on the "advice" of the Ministry of Defence. Later that year the NI Secretary, Roy Mason, accused the Corporation of disloyalty and suggested a three-month ban on reporting violence; he subsequently proposed an all-Ireland D-Notice system (see Chapter 8), a theme to which he returned in 1988.

In March 1977 Roy Mason and the Conservative Party condemned the BBC for transmitting (after a delay and investigation) allegations of RUC maltreatment of a teacher (who later proved his injuries in court). In December similar attacks followed a *Tonight* feature on the Republican movement. The pressure was not all coming from the UK; in May, Irish cabinet minister Conor Cruise O'Brien stated that he had complained to the BBC and ITV about IRA interviews.

In July 1979, the government of Mrs Thatcher had the first of several public clashes with the BBC over an interview with a spokesman for the INLA, which had earlier assassinated a leading Tory MP. The government considered prosecuting the BBC under the PTA for withholding information about the interviewee. Later in 1979 Granada TV's *World in Action* dropped an interview with a Sinn Féin leader after NI Secretary Humphrey Atkins refused to appear on the same programme; the Carrickmore affair (see below) occurred in the same year.

42

Allegations of left-wing bias in the BBC flew thick and fast in 1985, when it was persuaded to postpone and re-edit a documentary, *Real Lives*, on Republican leader Martin McGuinness, and DUP Councillor Gregory Campbell.

Following the shooting dead of three unarmed IRA members in Gibraltar in 1988, Thames TV's *This Week* team made a programme, "Death on the Rock", which challenged the official version of the incident. The government attempted to prevent its showing in the UK by alleging that it would prejudice an inquest in Gibraltar. The programme was shown as planned, as was a similar documentary in the BBC NI *Spotlight* series, both attracting a great deal of invective from the press and government. The programmes were banned in Gibraltar.

The government expressed such outrage that Thames felt the need to commission a special inquiry into the programme, and published the resulting report [22] as a paperback book. The report, the commissioning of which caused some misgivings among media professionals, vindicated the programme and presented a detailed and useful study of the law, practices and procedures affecting investigative journalism on TV.

Another censorship case based on the suggestion that broadcasts would prejudice a court hearing involved a Channel 4 project. The station proposed to film nightly re-enactments of ongoing proceedings in a December 1987 appeal against the conviction of the "Birmingham Six" whose claims to be innocent of IRA bombings had found widespread public support. The series was stopped by the Appeal Court on the grounds that it would undermine confidence in the legal system and so would amount to contempt of court.

43

Using journalism for intelligence purposes

On a number of occasions the unique position of journalists has been exploited, and severely jeopardised, by security forces

---

22> *The Windlesham-Rampton Report on Death on the Rock*, Faber and Faber, London, 1989

seeking to gather intelligence or prosecution evidence. Three forms of abuse are involved: the falsification of press credentials; seizing journalists' materials or forcing them to give evidence in person; and private pressure on journalists to pass on information. Each such incident creates difficulties for journalists by presenting them as proxy spies.

In 1972 RTE editor Kevin O'Kelly was imprisoned for three months, by a Dublin court, after refusing to identify the then chief-of-staff of the IRA, whom he had interviewed. BBC TV reporter Bernard Falk was jailed for four days in a similar case in Northern Ireland in 1971.

There were a number of reports around 1974-77 of undercover British Army personnel carrying faked press cards. After protests from the NUJ, and the shooting of one agent by the IRA, the practice apparently ceased. In 1988, however, an Army video crew observing a Republican procession told locals that they were working for a British television company. An apology was subsequently issued.

In November 1979 the BBC's *Panorama* programme filmed IRA activities in Carrickmore, Co. Tyrone. After sections of the press and some MPs condemned what they regarded as collusion in IRA propaganda, the untransmitted film was seized under the PTA; the editor was sacked by the BBC (but later reinstated) and the programme was abandoned.

In March 1988 two British Army corporals were shot dead after driving into a Republican funeral procession in Andersonstown. Some 27 photographers and journalists were subpoenaed to give evidence at the six ensuing trials and quantities of film, tape and prints were seized under the EPA. Two of those called to give evidence, BBC NI Head of News John Conway and reporter Korky Erskine, had death threats made against them and were removed to England for their own safety. The court forbade the publication of the names of most of the witnesses, or of court artists' sketches of them.

Attacks on prominent politicians

It is arguable that every politically-motivated killing, assault or threat is an act of censorship, in that it interferes with the rights of opinion and expression of the victim. A more clear-cut case is where the murder is that of an elected representative or party functionary; the probable intention is to prevent that person from communicating his or her views, and to intimidate others.

Since the commencement of the Troubles, most such attacks on politicians have been directed at those who were themselves members or supporters of violent groups (for example, the wounding of Gerry Adams MP, and the murders of Republicans Máire Drumm, Miriam Daly, Ronnie Bunting and Noel Little, and UDA leader John McMichael).

Several Unionist or Conservative personalities have been killed by the IRA or INLA (Senator Jack Barnhill 1971, Airey Neave MP 1975, Sir Norman Stronge and Robert Bradford MP 1981, Councillor Charles Armstrong and Edgar Graham 1983, Anthony Berry MP 1984, ex-Cllr George Seawright 1987, Colin Abernethy 1988) or wounded (John Taylor MP 1972, Cllr Joe Gaston 1975, Cllr Billy Dickson 1982, Cllr David Calvert 1987). A Fine Gael senator, Billy Fox, was murdered in the South in 1974.

On the Nationalist side, fewer have been killed by Loyalist paramilitaries (Senator Paddy Wilson 1973, Cllr John Turnly 1980, Cllr Lawrence Kennedy 1981, Cllr John Davey 1989) or injured (Bernadette McAliskey 1981). There have been many unsuccessful assassination attempts or conspiracies against both Nationalists (Frank McManus MP 1973) and Unionists (Thomas Passmore 1976, Rev. William Beattie 1982, Cllr Gregory Campbell and the Conservative leadership and Cabinet 1984, Jim Nicholson MP 1987, Ken Maginnis MP and William McCrea MP 1988).

There have been countless physical attacks and threats against the persons, family and property of non-violent political activists. Such incidents, together with the more serious assaults and the stress and inconvenience associated with maintaining personal security, provide a powerful deterrent against entering into or remaining in public life, and an incentive to "keep a low profile" which is self-censorship by another name.

Harassment of political activists

There are frequent reports, especially at election times and from the Republican camp, of security forces in Northern Ireland harassing, arresting and intimidating party workers in the course of distributing posters, papers and other promotional material, or maltreating them while in custody. Sinn Féin made many such allegations to the media in the course of the 1989 local government elections in Northern Ireland.

There is no easy way of independently establishing the truth or otherwise of most such claims, but there have been a few court cases: for example, SF councillor Noel Carroll was awarded damages in February 1988. (More than £315,000 was paid in the five years to April 1989 to 160 persons assaulted or wrongfully arrested or imprisoned by the Army and UDR, but the government refused to tell a Unionist MP how many of those involved were councillors, and would not give figures relating to claims against the RUC.) There have also been many army raids on SF premises, and occasional seizures of the party newspaper *Republican News*, especially in the 1970s.

The rights of expression of Irish political groups have also been interfered with in Britain; state action is generally limited to surveillance and infiltration, but unofficial groups frequently use violent tactics. There are many recorded instances of ultra-right groups such as the National Front, the British Movement and the British National Party launching attacks on Republican marches and meetings.

News management and disinformation

Both the state and the various paramilitary groups in Northern Ireland have been accused of falsifying information to obtain or influence media coverage. Disinformation or "black propaganda" activities, as distinct from the normal public relations activities of the state and private bodies, interfere with the public's right to receive information.

There is a grey area between disinformation and PR which might be termed news management, that is, the staging of events or the use of other power or influence to secure or affect media coverage. Whether this is an infringement of information rights is open to debate. The press, PR and advertising budget for the Northern Ireland Office currently stands at about £7.5 million per year; this is largely spent in routine publicity and information activities, but a proportion of it funds propaganda campaigns planned by "information policy" or "information strategy" groups.

By definition a successful disinformation effort is one which is never exposed as such, so that the only known examples are those which have been frustrated by disclosure. "Black propaganda" exercises, and "psyops" (psychological operations) by the Army and other security agencies reportedly occurred on a large scale especially in the period 1972-76, but continued into the 1980s.

Stories carried uncritically in the British press, with no factual basis and almost certainly "planted", included one in 1972 (after Bloody Sunday) about a supposed IRA plan to dress up as soldiers and shoot civil rights marchers. People were reported to be beating themselves up in police or army custody; a police surgeon who gave evidence to the contrary was slandered; the IRA was reported to be using 8-year-olds to throw bombs, hiring Czech hitmen, training in Libya, plotting to kidnap English villagers, and raping teenagers in Belfast; unarmed victims of some police army shootings were falsely reported to have been armed, or to have sped through non-existent roadblocks. At least three individuals named by papers as leading IRA terrorists in Britain were discovered living peacefully in Ireland. A libel on a Unionist leader was planted in a German magazine, fake Loyalist paramilitary groups were set up, and a mix of genuine and spurious intelligence data was supplied to the press and politicians.

47

News management could be said to include events such as that in 1979 when the BBC filmed the IRA "take-over" of Carrickmore. The journalists involved found themselves accused of having served as tools of the IRA, but had they failed to use the opportunity, they would have laid themselves open to charges of censorship. (That is perhaps the sort of moral dilemma that Mr Hurd had in mind when he maintained that broadcasters might prefer straightforward rules to having to decide what to do on a case-by-case basis.) On the government side, the preferred tactics are to secure coverage by staging media events and photo-opportunities designed to illustrate the government's commitment to the province and the "normalisation" of the situation; and, more questionably, to feed selected journalists with briefings to ensure that the government perspective is put without attribution. One instance (admitted by the UK Defence Secretary in March 1989) was the distribution of a document rubbishing a Thames TV documentary on the Gibraltar killings.

Other instances are rather different in that they concern the use of state power to grant access to information which would otherwise be unavailable. In the summer of 1989 the BBC screened a documentary series, *Families at War*, which included a lengthy interview with Shane Paul O'Doherty, then serving 30 life sentences for an IRA bombing campaign. The interview was clearly considered permissible, and transmissible, only because O'Doherty had renounced the IRA and violence. At about the same time, that is for the 20th anniversary of the arrival of British troops in Belfast and Derry, ITV was permitted to film a documentary (*For Queen and Country*) which dealt with the life of British troops in Northern Ireland, with apparently uncensored and somewhat robust views being expressed by the "squaddies". In both cases there must have been a political decision taken to permit access, presumably in the belief that the end product would further the objectives of the government.

48

The position of the Irish language

Many Unionists are inclined to view the Irish language - taught almost exclusively in Catholic schools, rather than state schools - as something subversive. The language is not widely spoken and survives mainly in transliterated place-names and personal names; there are no longer any legal penalties for its use in Northern Ireland, but those who seek to use it encounter certain problems.

Those who use the historic Gaelic spellings of their personal names, rather than anglicised versions, find that unfavourable assumptions are made by prospective employers and security force personnel about their political orientation. Occasional prolonged and hostile questioning as to one's "real" name is the least inconvenience that may be expected. Prisoners have been refused permission to correspond in Irish or to have Irish bibles. It is still the law that local authorities may not erect bilingual street or road signs.

Problems also arise in relation to access to the media. Some NI newspapers such as the *Coleraine Chronicle* and the *Northern Constitution* have a policy of censoring any Irish words; others which have allowed the occasional phrase to appear in an unremarkable context, for example the September 1989 use of the words *fleadh cheoil* (an Irish music festival) in the Belfast *Sunday News*, have published complaints from readers appalled at the intrusion of "alien" expressions into columns which ought to be devoted exclusively to "the Queen's English".

There is some cause for optimism, however. Registrars of births no longer routinely alter Irish forenames to "acceptable" spellings, as used to be the practice, and there appears to be an increasing awareness of the desirability of recognising and respecting the diverse cultural inheritances of the two communities.

Other informal censorship

Throughout the decades of self-rule in Northern Ireland members of the Westminster Parliament observed a convention of ignoring the "internal" affairs of the province. Under direct rule Westminster has become the only parliamentary forum for Northern Ireland and there are numerous, if rarely well-attended, debates and speeches on its problems. However, the damaging legacy of the fifty-year silence may be seen in the new convention that important legislation for the province is implemented by means of Order in Council, which restricts debate and allows for no amendments. The 17 Northern MPs are rarely able to determine the outcome of any vote and there is nothing akin to the Scottish MP's Grand Council which functioned as a sort of provincial senate.

It has been argued that the continuing refusal of the main British political parties to permit the formation of branches

49

within Northern Ireland, despite their professed commitment to the Union and despite the reported wishes of a large section of the province's population, constitutes a form of censorship in that it prevents the policies of the parties which rule the province from being placed officially before the local electorate, and prevents those ruled by those parties from informing and influencing party policy.

5. SELF-CENSORSHIP

The term "self-censorship" has arisen to describe cases where writers and media personnel either refrain from covering sensitive topics or opt to cover them in a restricted way, other than as a result of censorship imposed from above. Examples would be an over-zealous exclusion of dissent from RTE television programmes beyond that demanded by Section 31, or a newspaper's decision to refrain from publishing IRA statements in the interests of "depriving terrorism of a platform".

Self-censorship may operate only momentarily, within the mind of a journalist, in which case it may be quite voluntary and may be motivated by some concept of "responsible journalism"; or it may acquire a life of its own either as a strategy to preserve one's job or as an aspect of the editorial function within a media organisation. It may then be imposed by senior editors or managers, or by broadcasting authorities, on lower-ranking journalists and programme-makers.

It is important to understand that the term is not strictly accurate. The self is not censored; what is censored is information, and the victim is not so much the journalist, nor the person or group whose views go unreported, as the information requirement of the intended audience. Self-censorship is thus as effective and pernicious as any other form of censorship. To withhold political information voluntarily, even when it is not legally necessary to do so, is to impoverish democracy by disabling debate. In Ireland today it is very possible that irresponsible self-censorship, by impeding rational debate, prolongs armed conflict: careless silence, then, can cost lives.

Self-censorship is peculiarly difficult to diagnose or document. The first problem is in distinguishing between it and the duty of editors and journalists to provide analysis and interpretation of what they see as important in the whole range

51

of current events: they have no duty to report only the bare facts, nor to report all the facts, nor to draw clear lines between news, news analysis and comment. Their purpose is not to compile a vast catalogue of events but to select from them and to explain their context and significance: thus an element of selectivity and weighting, or bias, is actually required of the media, and in principle one should be able to choose the medium which most nearly corresponds to one's own information needs, world-view and priorities.

The second problem is that, even in the complete absence of government interference, market forces militate against a free press. There are political dimensions to the relationship of journalist with news medium, and of medium with owner. The journalist is more likely to find his/her work printed if it starts from a political perspective aligned with that of the medium, so s/he may toe the line; if unconsciously, is it self-censorship? By extension, should a medium which ignores views outside its political perspective be regarded as self-censoring? It is a universal truth that media owners - including governments - lay down standards or objectives for their media (possibly including broad support for a particular party or for the "middle ground"); management and senior editors are required to formulate and impose policy as to news priorities and political lines, and sub-editors and journalists are hired on the expectation that they will operate effectively within such policy. Private media proprietors are usually wealthy individuals or groups whose interests coincide with mainstream political parties, and it is reasonable to expect their interests to be reflected in the product of their media. That is certainly the case in Britain, and to some extent in Ireland. To suggest that it is somehow unfair for, say, a Conservative newspaper to edit or refuse a Marxist journalist's analysis of government policies is to suggest that newspapers have no right to be Conservative. The broadcasting oligopoly is a different case: whereas people choose from the many newspapers according to their political orientation, the public in Britain and Ireland expect something close to impartiality of the broadcast media.

The third problem is in distinguishing between censorship required by law and that which oversteps the minimum legal requirements. That applies not just to those monitoring the operation of the law but to journalists and editors obliged to work within it: from the day the UK broadcasting ban was announced, Home Office advice and legal opinion has been sought on many occasions as to what may or may not be heard. The uncertainties arising from imprecise terminology in the relevant legislation and executive orders have inevitably led some broadcasters to err on the side of caution; that may, of course, have been foreseen and intended when the drafting took place.

Finally, there is real difficulty in persuading some of those who exercise it to acknowledge that self-censorship exists. Members of the NUJ have a Code of Conduct, several clauses of which are concerned with defending freedom of the press, accuracy and refusal to suppress or distort the facts. This public rejection of self-censorship makes it difficult for journalists to admit, even in private, that it occurs at all. It is thus impossible to quantify the extent of self-censorship.

Discussion of the ways in which self-censorship may arise from or affect the Irish Troubles should be mindful of Holmes' dog: often the absence of barking is the true indicator that all is not well. In relation to the press and broadcasting industries of the Republic of Ireland and Great Britain, the truly remarkable feature of their reportage and analysis of the Northern Ireland conflict is that there is so little of it.

53

The newsworthiness of an event may be directly proportional to the distance at which it occurs from the headquarters of the media institutions. Northern Ireland is no longer a story. It rarely makes the front page of British newspapers, or the lead item in TV or radio news, unless some atrocity has occurred. In addition to the difficulties of covering a province of which they know little, British broadcasters now have to cope with editors, managers and ultimately the government looking over their shoulders, to ensure that their work stays on the right side of the new censorship rules. Far easier, if one is planning a documentary series or even a lengthy news feature, to consider a less contentious theme.

Broadcasting in the UK

It is difficult to say at what point the "referral upwards" system which has evolved in both commercial and public broadcasting in reporting Northern Ireland [23] ceases to be voluntary self-censorship by ITV, the BBC or their constituent parts, and becomes informal censorship resulting from behind-the-scenes government pressure (covered in Chapter 6); that is particularly the case when the relevant decision is taken at the highest level, meaning, in the UK, at the top of the BBC or by the IBA (formerly ITA). In any case its effect is to inhibit reporting of news and current affairs by requiring prior authority for what would otherwise be within the discretion of individual journalists and programme-makers.

Pre-ban self-censorship by the UK broadcasting authorities

Given the centrality of Republican ideology to the dynamics of the Irish Troubles, and the role of Sinn Féin as the main legally-constituted exponent of that ideology, one might expect the national broadcast media to take frequent opportunities to present and analyse SF policies and activities. According to the Shadow Home Secretary, ITV broadcast a total of just four minutes of interviews with SF members in the year before the broadcasting ban came into effect. Since there was no legal obstacle it would seem that voluntary restraint by the broadcasting authority and companies was operating to a degree that would suggest that the ban was superfluous.

That restraint has mainly operated invisibly and by consent of most of those in the industry; Roger Gale MP (Cons.), a former broadcast journalist, has said that "historically there has been a clear understanding among [broadcasters] that you do not give promotional airtime to terrorists" [24]. However, in the course of the past 20 years there have been several occasions when the caution of senior staff has exceeded that of their juniors, resulting in executive intervention to alter or stop

54

23> see Curtis 1984
24> *The Times* 20.10.88

sensitive programmes. These cases are self-censorship only insofar as the censorship arose within the broadcasting organisations concerned.

In 1970 the BBC commissioned a play about Northern Ireland by Jim Allen (later the author of the controversial play *Perdition*). The corporation abandoned the project during writing.

In 1971 the BBC considered whether to ban the broadcast of interviews with Irish Republicans, but opted instead for "a scrupulous editorial watch" over reporting the North and a firm policy of "balance"; IRA interviews could be recorded with prior permission from senior management, but from April 1971 that permission was almost always withheld and the rule was later extended to Loyalist paramilitaries [25].

There were only three IRA interviews on the BBC in 1971, one in 1972, none at all in 1973, one in 1974 and none in 1975-84; the INLA was interviewed twice, in 1977 and 1979. Independent TV never interviewed the INLA and carried perhaps six IRA interviews. Even the legal groups affected by the 1988 ban appeared very infrequently in broadcasts. Those 13 years of a virtual ban included the bloodiest phases of the Troubles, with some 2,400 deaths.

In August 1971 the BBC prevented its *24 Hours* series from making a programme about the history of the IRA; in September it failed to transmit an interview with an ex-internee, Michael Farrell, about prison conditions; and in November the ITA banned a Granada *World in Action* programme including IRA and SF interviews on the assertion of ITA Chairman Lord Aylestone that it would be "aiding and abetting the enemy". In the same year Independent Television News (ITN) refused to transmit a report on Derry city, and the BBC delayed another *24 Hours* feature about maltreatment of internees.

The IBA viewed a Dominic Behan play, *The Folk Singer*, before authorising its transmission in November 1972; it was broadcast at a later hour than non-Irish plays in the same series. In the same month the BBC refused to show a film,

55

25>   see Schlesinger 1987

A Sense of Loss, which it had co-financed; the explanation was that the film was "too pro-Irish". In 1975 the IBA postponed a *This Week* report on IRA fund-raising on the grounds that "the subject matter could have an unfortunate impact on opinions and emotions"; the implications are (a) that it is the subject matter, rather than the content, of a broadcast which is sensitive, and (b) that the TV authorities have the duty and ability to distinguish between factual programmes with a "fortunate" or "unfortunate" impact on "opinions and emotions".

In 1976 the BBC banned a play by Brian Phelan, *Article 5*, because it referred in passing to Northern Ireland as a place where torture was used by a government; in 1977 it refused to transmit a commissioned documentary on the Short Strand area of Belfast. Also in 1977 the IBA banned a Thames *This Week* report on Queen Elizabeth's visit to Northern Ireland, just two minutes before transmission; it was shown days later after some cuts were made. The reporter involved, Peter Taylor, had another NI documentary project rejected in 1978 by Thames and the BBC.

In May 1978 a documentary on the IRA in London Weekend TV's *Weekend World* series was banned by the IBA, but an altered version was allowed to be shown three weeks late. A *This Week* report on the Amnesty International investigation of RUC interrogations was banned by the IBA in June. In August the BBC showed a much-delayed and altered *Play for Today* about a bombing trial.

In May 1979 the IBA, responding to protests from MPs, ordered the removal of an SF interview from David Frost's *Global Village*. Yorkshire TV acquiesced. In August the BBC cancelled a play, *The Vanishing Army*, because of the Warrenpoint and Mountbatten killings. A March 1980 BBC2 documentary about British soldiers was denounced in the House of Commons, so the BBC banned repeats and foreign sales. In the same year, responding to the Carrickmore incident (see Chapter 6), the BBC cancelled another *Panorama* on the IRA and tightened up its "referral upwards" system; controversial programmes on Northern Ireland were

56

thereafter referred as high as the Board of Governors, which has since 1985 claimed the right to over-rule the BBC management on such issues.

The IBA demanded a 33-second cut in a Thames *TV Eye* film on the hunger strikes in April 1981. In June Granada withdrew its *World in Action* programme, "The propaganda war", rather than make a similar cut ordered by the IBA. In September the BBC appeared to subscribe to an alternative logic to that of the 1988 ban in deciding that factual images, rather than opinionated voices, conveyed most offence: they refused to show a video on *Top of the Pops* which illustrated a song by *Police* with shots of Belfast street scenes.

BBC2's *Open Door* access slot proved not quite open enough for the Campaign for Free Speech on Ireland, which won approval for a programme in November 1979 but was banned from making it in January 1982. In October 1983 a Channel 4 film, *The Cause of Ireland*, had six minutes excised at the insistence of the IBA.

The censorship controversy arising from the *Real Lives* documentary in 1985 is discussed in Chapter 6.

Pre-ban self-censorship by UK local television companies

In July 1966 Ulster Television (UTV) refused to show a networked *This Week* programme which presented an unflattering portrait of Rev. Ian Paisley. In June 1968, despite considerable internal debate, BBC Northern Ireland refused to make a programme about the Dungannon housing dispute which was central to the development of the civil rights movement, and for two days in August 1969 it anticipated the 1988 ban by deciding not to transmit actuality broadcasts of "sectarian opinion".

In July 1970 BBC NI refused to transmit a *Panorama* programme on the Troubles. In February 1971 NI Controller Waldo Maguire delayed a *24 Hours* programme on dissent within the Unionist Party until the resignation of the then NI Prime Minister made the film redundant; and later that year the BBC filmed, but never transmitted, the proceedings of a

Nationalist "alternative parliament". The next year Maguire persuaded BBC Controller of TV David Attenborough to delay transmission of a Dominic Behan play, *Carson Country*, until after the province's summer "marching season".

In February 1973 Sir Lew Grade, head of ATV, banned Kenneth Griffith's film biography of the long-dead Southern leader Michael Collins. Another Griffith documentary on Ireland was banned by Harlech TV in March 1980. In October 1976 a BBC Scotland documentary had an IRA interview excised at the insistence of the Controller NI but a UDA interview was left in. In 1978 BBC NI forced changes to two programmes in a documentary series, *The Irish Way*; the director resigned. In August 1978 UTV dropped an Ulster-set episode from an Army drama series, *Spearhead*.

A singularly vivid example of the rationale of self-censorship arose in November 1979, when a BBC NI *Spotlight* discussion of the Carrickmore *Panorama* incident was cancelled because the Corporation's higher management would not provide someone to represent it and "balance" the discussion: the BBC thus found itself censoring a BBC programme about a censored BBC programme, because of the BBC's refusal to appear on the BBC.

A delayed, cut and altered Thames film, *Creggan*, was screened in June 1980 and won great praise, but it has been refused repeat showings. In March 1983 Yorkshire TV stopped a *First Tuesday* documentary on plastic bullets after pressure from the RUC and the IBA. In the same year Channel 4 dropped an *Eleventh Hour* feature, "The Cause of Ireland"; it withdrew Gerry Adams' invitation to appear on *Right to Reply* after the Harrods bombing; and most absurdly, it dropped Irish passages from its *Comedy Classics* series featuring Norman Wisdom, Paul Hogan and others.

In 1984 Yorkshire dropped Adams from the Jimmy Young chat show, and Channel 4 repeatedly delayed a film, *Green Flutes*, about Glasgow Irish bands. In 1985 a *Panorama* on the shoot-to-kill controversy was delayed for a year in all, and has not been repeated despite winning a Royal Television Society award. BBC2's *Newsnight* declined a CBS report about the *Real Lives* case, and BBC Scotland withdrew an invitation to Adams to appear on *Open to Question*. The BBC postponed an

Open Space feature made by Loyalist and Republican prisoners' families; UTV cut a five-minute sequence from its religious programme *Witness*, ITV cancelled the broadcast of a Midnight Mass from a Belfast hospital and the BBC cancelled a *Songs of Praise* from Dungannon because of Protestant objections.

In 1986 the BBC cancelled a *Question Time* from Belfast, and stopped its live coverage of the 12th July marches; Channel 4 dropped a 12-minute video commissioned from Belfast children and dealing with plastic bullet killings. 1987 was a better year, but in 1988 Channel 4 postponed a film, *Acceptable Levels*, solely because it coincided with the Birmingham Six appeal; the same station withdrew Gerry Adams' invitation to appear on a late-night talk show after other guests objected.

Broadcasting under the UK ban

There is just one sense in which the 1988 ban could have had a beneficial effect on broadcast coverage of Northern Ireland. Whereas the instances cited above of national and local interference and censorship of one kind or another were somewhat unpredictable, subjective and arbitrary, the ban systematised the censorship and set out its legal, administrative and ideological basis. Before the ban programme-makers never knew at what level, or on what grounds, their approach would cause offence and bring in the censors: now at least they can be sure that certain types of approach are not permitted, and if they were sufficiently courageous they could use the specificity of the ban as implying a blanket permission to cover topics and individuals not expressly covered by it. Moreover the formalisation of what were hitherto vague taboos provided a better opportunity for mounting an effective challenge to the restrictions.

Some, including the British Home Secretary, Douglas Hurd, went so far as to suggest that the ban would actually be welcomed by broadcasters:[26]

26>   *Hansard* 19.10.88

From their point of view it is more clear and straightforward... to operate under a notice of this sort, for which I take responsibility and which the House will debate, than to have to operate at their discretion, sometimes in difficult circumstances... What it does is to state clearly and precisely an obligation with which the broadcasters have been wrestling, case by case and programme by programme, with some difficulty for many years... As they reflect on it they will see that this gives them a clearer and better way to proceed than they ever had.

In fact while the ban's restrictions have been rigorously enforced, there has been no concomitant relaxation in dealing with controversial topics or persons outside its terms. The effect has been quite the reverse. The ban has been given an over-wide interpretation in practice, and broadcasters have become ever more cautious in all their activities in relation to the province.

Apart from the continuing paucity of coverage of Northern Ireland since the imposition of the 1988 ban, which could be ascribed to all sorts of reasons other than disinclination on the part of programme- makers, self-censorship may be evident in the subjects or approaches adopted or avoided in those programmes which are screened. There has been a consistent unwillingness to test the ban to the legal limits, and a willingness to censor far beyond the requirements of the ban.

No broadcast journalist has yet gone on record as approving of the ban. On the other hand, none seem to have openly disobeyed it; that is only evidence of self-censorship if the concept can reasonably be extended to the failure to do illegal things rather than the failure to exercise freedoms available within the law. That may be the view of the 10 Labour MPs who signed a Commons motion stating that there was no duty to obey this "unjust law".

The press office of Sinn Féin in Belfast has reported a 75 per cent decline in UK broadcast media enquiries since the ban

60

was imposed, and other radical Nationalist "media personalities" say that their invitations to appear on BBC or IBA programmes have declined markedly.

A failure of imagination

The easiest way for broadcasters to register a lawful protest at the ban is for them to observe it to the letter, which means employing their creativity and the best legal advice to find ways of maintaining their previous level of coverage of the affected organisations. Their approach to date has been unimaginative: there have been few attempts to test the limits of the ban, and the extra work involved in preparing pre-recorded material for transmission appears to have operated as a real disincentive. The public is denied all actuality coverage of the opinions of paramilitary apologists, even in the aftermath of incidents which would provide an opportunity to question their political sincerity or the morality of their strategy, and in the permitted reportage of their statements news value, nuances of tone and phrase, and part of the meaning are lost through delay, precis and paraphrase.

The biggest loophole in the 1988 ban was quickly spotted, and confirmed by the Home Office: broadcasters have the freedom to use film of the words being spoken, with verbatim or paraphrase voice-over. Moreover, Home Office guidance stated [27] that actors in a work of fiction were not covered.

Broadcasters have generally failed to take advantage of the loopholes. While there has been some use of the paraphrase voice-over, they have only rarely "lip-synched" the actual utterances of banned individuals. There is nothing in the ban, and no real technological problem, to prevent them doing so with either live or pre-recorded material, so long as the voice of the interviewee cannot be heard. Alternatively, questions could be put orally to a banned person and answered laboriously in writing by him live on screen. At the very least, all news reports on Northern Ireland which would ordinarily have contained material now banned could be prefaced with a

61

27> letter 24.10.88, from Head of Broadcasting Dept. to BBC

phrase based on that which is invariably used to introduce reports from South Africa: "This report has been compiled under the government-imposed reporting restrictions".

The fiction exemption would allow the broadcast of otherwise banned opinion with impunity in a dramatic context: it would be permissible, if politically impossible, to broadcast from a fictional setting, say a press conference, with actors expounding the actual views and policies of the affected organisations.

Broadcasters as thought police

One of the most disquieting aspects of the operation of the ban in both countries is that it requires broadcasters to police the airwaves to prevent forbidden opinions from slipping out. It is relatively easy to identify official spokespersons for the affected organisations, but how can one anticipate that a prospective interviewee might utter an illegal phrase?

A logical consequence of an enthusiastic approach to enforcement - and it has not been possible to establish just what has been done to date by any station or network - would be for broadcasting organisations, perhaps in association with a state or private security agency, to compile and circulate blacklists of people who are unsafe to have on live programmes. It is unlikely that those placed on such blacklists would be informed of the fact or allowed an appeal. Phone-ins would be fewer in number. Live person-in-the-street interviewing in strongly Loyalist or Republican areas would be avoided. Studio audience participation in talk shows may be restricted. This might at first appear fanciful but RTE journalists, who have laboured under their ban for almost two decades, are required, under guidelines, to ask polential interviewees whether they are members of Sinn Féin. Vetting of studio audiences is routine.

Those who have views which coincide even slightly with those of a banned organisation - for example, British people in favour of withdrawal from Ireland - have found themselves subject to interrogation about the nature and extent of their sympathies, and they may then be refused access to radio or TV (see the case of Cllr Richard Stanton of Brighton,

Chapter 9). Over time, the blacklists will grow and a surreal "consensus" will emerge in all live broadcasts: too bad for anyone who tunes in in the hope of hearing intelligent and informed debate.

The first clumsy attempts at vetting took place within a day of the ban being imposed. Sinn Féin's London representative, Gerry Mac Lochlainn, answered truthfully that he did not "vote for" the party (which does not put up candidates in London), and so was allowed to appear illegally on BBC TV's *Kilroy* chat show.

Application of restrictions not required by the ban

From the day the ban was imposed, 19th October 1988, there were explicit suggestions that broadcasters had a public duty to apply it beyond what the law required.

The BBC news at 1 p.m. that day carried an interview with Gerry Adams, president of Sinn Féin. The ban had not yet been announced and had not come into force, so the interview might have been considered a timely and proper piece of journalism. Nevertheless, it came in for severe criticism: the *Daily Express,* quoting Tory MP Ivor Stanbrook and an anonymous minister, said the BBC was "under fire for beating the ban"; the *Daily Star* said "furious MPs blasted the BBC for allowing Adams to beat the ban", quoting the same furious MP, as did *The Sun* which claimed that "BBC bosses stuck two fingers up at the government". Stanbrook said "It shows you can't rely on the media to behave responsibly by self-discipline", the implication being that the media needed to be bound by laws.

63

Not all sections of the Corporation were feeling defiant that day: Radio WM, the Birmingham local station, dropped an interview with SF general secretary Tom Hartley some hours before the ban took effect.

From the Home Office [28] there came a suggestion that for the broadcasters to use a voice-over on statements, which had

28> *The Guardian* 20.10.88

earlier been acknowledged as being lawful, would be "against the spirit of the ban". In suggesting that broadcasters ought to act in the "spirit" of the ban, the government was clearly endorsing self-censorship.

The ban applies only to the BBC and the IBA, but cable and satellite broadcasters were quoted from the day of its inception as saying that they would "comply with" it, meaning that they would voluntarily self-censor. The Cable Authority, responsible for regulating that sector, later stated officially that its operators would have to consider themselves bound by the ban "because we are not keen for cable to be manipulated as a loophole"; when a US-based news service, CNN, expressed misgivings, the Authority threatened to "take them out of the cable network" [29].

On the day the ban was announced, Birmingham radio station BMRB became the first of many stations to drop a planned phone-in programme in case the *vox pop* contributions included some illegal opinions. BMRB also decided not to interview former MP Bernadette McAliskey, not a member of any of the 11 affected groups but a radical Nationalist whose opinions coincide to some extent with the policies of Sinn Féin.

The BBC has transmitted interviews with London Labour MP Ken Livingstone and US Senator Edward Kennedy, both of whom were mentioned in an internal memo in November 1988 as potentially affected by the ban because of their sympathies with Irish Nationalist aspirations. The memo arose from discussions on "guidelines" produced by the Corporation's Head of Editorial Policy, John Wilson, and Head of News, Ron Neil, which reportedly went well beyond the terms of the ban.

In the same month County Sound Radio in Hampshire cancelled an interview with a member of a pressure group seeking to reopen the case of the Guildford Four (imprisoned for an IRA bombing in 1974).

64

29> *Sunday Telegraph* 23.10.88

Subversive singing

The banning of songs with Irish political references is nothing new: the BBC has prohibited the playing of John Lennon's early 1970s song "Give Ireland back to the Irish", and very few of the partisan ballads to have emerged from the Troubles have ever been broadcast. However, since the 1988 ban its provisions against the solicitation of support for specified organisations have been applied to any song with a tenuous connection with the causes espoused by those bodies; it has now become a vehicle for censorship of dissident artistic expression.

A particularly worrying example, because it demonstrated the willingness of the IBA to decree a unilateral extension of the terms of the ban, concerns "Streets of Sorrow", a ballad by Irish group *The Pogues*. An IBA circular in November 1988 said that the song, sympathetic to the "Birmingham Six", should not be broadcast because it "indicate[s] a general disagreement with the way the government responds to, and the courts deal with, the terrorist threat". Neither *The Pogues* nor the Six have expressed support for any of the banned groups.

In a similar case, London independent radio station LBC refused on 8th November to play a *Dubliners* recording of a famous ballad, "Kelly the Boy from Killane", dating from the United Irish rebellion of 1798; it would appear that two centuries are not enough to reduce the potency of some lyrics.

It has even been reported that broadcasters have agonised over the transmission of crowd noise from football matches - for example, Glasgow Celtic v Rangers - where Republican or Loyalist songs or chants could be expected.

65

Broadcasting in the Irish Republic

The Section 31 ban on "subversives" having their speech reported, let alone broadcast, is so sweeping that there are not many opportunities for journalists to choose freely whether to disseminate or censor a particular item of information. As in the UK, it is easier to point to the lack of reportage of the NI situation than it is to document instances of self-censorship.

As also in the UK, self-censorship predated the legal requirement by many years and continues to have an effect well beyond the letter of the law.

In 1964 RTE withheld a documentary, *Radharc in Derry*, on discrimination against Catholics in the North, on the grounds that it would be "unhelpful" to show it at a time when the then Taoiseach, Sean Lemass, was engaged in a rapprochement with the Unionist provincial government under Terence O'Neill.

The documentary was finally shown on 6th September 1989, and was followed by a rather dull studio discussion which dwelt almost exclusively on the way things had changed in Derry rather than on the politics of censorship. The suggestion was, however, made by panellist Eamonn McCann that RTE then and now was reluctant to focus honestly on the issues behind the conflict in the North; he decried "the failure of RTE to describe accurately and account for the mutual loathing of working-class Catholics and the RUC", alleging that "the whole picture is distorted in the interests of responsible broadcasting". The presenter, Pat Butler, ended by asking rhetorically how many other RTE films had been shelved. The fact is, of course, that only RTE knows the answer, but it does not discuss banned programmes nor its guidelines for staff as to what may or may not be said on air.

66

An RTE journalist has described the editorial impact of Section 31 thus: "The ultra-cautious atmosphere which Section 31 and the guidelines have fostered in the newsroom and programme sections has meant that inquiries into controversial issues have not been encouraged. Establishment views are aired at great length, often without analysis or counterpoint." RTE's Northern editor Jim Dougal was particularly frustrated at being unable to interview Republican leaders after the Enniskillen bombing, and he voiced the unhappiness felt by UK journalists at being forced to work for the government in keeping Sinn Féin views off the air. [30]

30> *The Guardian* 20.10.88

Self-censorship in print

Newspapers and other media in the UK are already routinely and voluntarily censored by means of the D-Notice system, whereby a joint government and media "Defence Press and Broadcasting Committee" advises editors of topics which may not be addressed on the grounds of national security. The D-Notice system, which has probably had some effect on the coverage of the NI conflict, can be bypassed but the new official secrets law will make it largely redundant by introducing legal sanctions in place of voluntary restraint. (One of the eight current notices asks that nothing be published about the operational methods of the British security and intelligence services, such as telephone tapping, discussed in Chapter 6.)

It remains to be seen whether the present British government will take the view that it would be helpful to newspaper editors, as they feel it is for broadcasters, to have censorship rules set out by means of a statute or executive order. Certainly the Home Secretary appears to believe that self-censorship is required now. Tory MP Robert Hughes put it to him in the October banning debate that "the British people look to the editors of newspapers voluntarily to understand that they do not want newspapers to be used as a platform for the IRA and its apologists". Mr Hurd replied: "The press certainly has a responsibility, just as the broadcasters have."

Even *The Sunday Times* has implied that journalists have a duty to self-censor: a recent article by defence correspondent James Adams, entitled "How the press plays into the terrorists' hands", described alleged manipulation of the media and ended: "It is the media which have to put their own house in order."

Once again, the main evidence of ongoing self-censorship is the low level of coverage which UK papers have given to the Troubles. Aside from the various anniversaries, when extensive and ill-informed comment can be guaranteed, Northern Ireland news is relegated to the inner pages and condensed to the point of evaporation.

The British readership, which foots the bill for the Troubles and is entitled to be kept informed, is thus taken quite unawares by events, such as the election to the Westminster Parliament of Bobby Sands on hungerstrike, a logical development for those following the story from closer at hand. Another criticism often made of the press in Britain and the Republic is its hyping of "good news" stories, such as job creation, the Peace People movement and the widely-chronicled exploits of a British Army dog .

In February 1986 Jo Thomas was recalled from the London bureau of *The New York Times* when she started to investigate NI "shoot-to-kill" cases. [31]

Whether any of this is strictly self-censorship is hard to state; it may just be the different news values which operate at a comfortable distance from the arena, or it may be due to "news management" (see Chapter 5). It may simply be that because violence has become "normal", non-violence stories are more newsworthy.

68

6. INTERCEPTION & SURVEILLANCE OF COMMUNICATIONS

The right to freedom of information is closely related to the right to privacy of the person, and more particularly of communication. In what the Universal Declaration defines as the freedom "to seek, receive and impart information and ideas" there is implicit the freedom to do so privately or publicly, without state supervision or intervention. There can be no "free" communication if it is liable to be scrutinised, recorded, delayed, withheld, altered or destroyed by a third party.

Very little has been published about the extent to which private communications in, or related to, Northern Ireland are the subject of attention by the authorities, but few commentators doubt that the mails and telecommunication systems are subject to massive routine surveillance and occasional interference. The lack of verifiable information means that this chapter can only discuss what might be happening, and under what legal authority. Certainly the legal powers, the facilities and the technology are available, and it seems improbable that they would not be extensively deployed in the interests of the anti-terrorist effort. There are three levels of possible activity.

69

Traffic analysis

The purpose of monitoring the flow of communications, as opposed to directly interfering with them, is to build up background intelligence on the activities and contacts of persons and organisations, and to collect information which may be analysed later in a more specific investigation. Two examples will illustrate the usefulness to the state of what is called "traffic analysis", "call logging" or "metering" in relation to telecommunications (including telex, telegram and fax, but mainly voice telephone traffic).

Firstly, by noting the frequency and source or destination of calls to or from a particular telephone, one can assess the subscriber's political affiliation and his or her place in the hierarchy of the organisations concerned. Secondly, by retrospectively analysing such flows one can work out who called someone just before something else happened; for example, what telephone was used to convey a paramilitary communiqué to a news agency.

The replacement of older telephone exchanges in Northern Ireland, and indeed in the rest of these islands, will enable security agencies to link directly into the computers which handle telephone traffic in the "System X" and later digital exchanges, without the need for physical placement of metering devices at some point on the lines. Whereas the old system meant that only a limited number of lines could be analysed, and physical evidence was present, the new system means that data relating to any telephone and any period of time can be retrieved quickly and unobtrusively.

Traffic analysis on a massive scale can be as useful to a security agency as actually listening in to telephone calls, and has the added advantage that it is subject to very little legal regulation because communications are not listened to or interfered with: only the "externals", meaning source, destination, time and so on, are considered, and a court is obliged to accept a ministerial statement citing national security as justifying the metering of any particular line.

In relation to mails, nothing of value can be extracted from looking at postal packets unless the sender gives a correct name and address or some other significant wording on the outside. The only exception is in monitoring outgoing mail, if it is possible to identify the sender.

Interception

By interception is meant actually listening to and/or recording telephone calls, and opening mails. The term can also cover electronic eavesdropping on private conversations, on computer screens or on other forms of communication.

Telephone tapping covers a variety of activities, from the screening or "trawling" of large numbers of calls (which can be done automatically) to pick up particular words or phrases, to the recording of every call to or from a particular number, from anywhere along the line or from a distance. It includes telephone-based bugging systems capable of picking up sounds throughout a room or building. The technology available as of the mid-1980s is described in Fitzgerald and Leopold 1987 (see Sources); the main point, as with traffic analysis, is that the procedures are very much easier after the introduction of programmable digital systems where just a few key-strokes at a Telecom operations centre will connect a third line, instantly and invisibly, to a two-way conversation.

Although UK law on telephone tapping was supposedly formalised in 1985 with an Interception of Communications Act (prompted by a European Court case, *Malone v UK*), the Act exempts official interception from any penalties provided that it occurs under a ministerial warrant. Each warrant can be used for a very large number of taps and can be renewed indefinitely.

71

Concerning Northern Ireland, the Act would seem to allow for a single warrant to authorise the tapping of the telephones of every member of a particular party or group and of anyone likely to speak to any member. The government consistently refuses to issue statistics on tapping in the province, and those issued on the rest of the UK are of little use given the scope of each warrant and the probability of unauthorised tapping.

The Army is thought to have been the main tapping agency in Northern Ireland at least into the 1970s. The microwave trunk lines across the Irish border are said to be monitored by army bases on Divis Mountain, near Belfast, and Clooney Park, Derry. The domestic security agency, MI5, is also said to be involved, and the RUC Special Branch would probably handle any tapping at local exchange level. According to Fitzgerald and Leopold, The Secret Intelligence Service - MI6 - co- operates with the signals intelligence agency, GCHQ, in running a microwave telephone tapping unit from inside the British Embassy in Dublin. (A similar MI5 scheme was referred to by Peter Wright in *Spycatcher*.) This assertion has not been contradicted and there appears to be no lawful basis for such activity in another country.

The IRA, and presumably other paramilitary groupings, have also resorted to telephone tapping, though infrequently and by means of old-fashioned "hard-wiring" to particular lines or street junction boxes.

Opening mails - or examining the contents without opening, for example by photographing letters against special lights - is one of the oldest forms of intelligence activity and it would be surprising if it did not happen extensively. There is much anecdotal evidence. It has been said that the technology is now so sophisticated that letters which arrive open are less likely to have been the subject of security attention than those which are intact.

In the UK, successive Post Office Acts since 1711 have authorised government ministers to issue warrants permitting the opening of mail. It is unlikely, however, that most of the interception is conducted under the cumbersome procedures of the current 1969 Act; a great deal of it may have been happening informally, but an easier legal instrument has now become available.

It is possible for anyone acting under the authority of the 1989 Prevention of Terrorism Act to open and examine letters provided that they satisfy a justice of the peace that they are doing so in the course of a "terrorist investigation": the permissions issued under the PTA cover not only known documents in a specified location, but material "expected to become available" to a stated address within 28 days. Security agencies with access to postal sorting offices and armed with a list of addresses would then be allowed under monthly-renewable warrants to open and read every piece of mail sent to those addresses. Such activities may well have gone on for many years before legal authority was granted by the PTA.

In the Republic of Ireland the Minister for Justice is authorised by statute to issue a warrant allowing the opening of post addressed to a named person, and custom and practice also allows the Minister to issue such warrants to cover telephone taps. Present arrangements for telephone tapping have been acknowledged to be in violation of the European Convention on Human Rights following the European Court's judgement on the similar UK arrangements (Malone Case). However, no legislation to provide safeguards against abuse has yet been introduced in the Oireachtas. The Dail has been assured that warrants are only signed when necessary for preventing or detecting crime, or to safeguard national security, but no statistics have been issued and some flagrant abuses have come to light.

There were persistent rumours of widespread tapping in the last months of 1982. It was revealed by journalist Peter Murtagh that those affected included two political columnists, Geraldine Kennedy and Bruce Arnold, and it later emerged that a Cabinet Minister was also tapped. The then Fianna Fail Justice Minister, Sean Doherty, a former policeman, was forced to resign from the Cabinet when the facts were revealed. The Garda Commissioner and his deputy also resigned. The journalists were awarded damages by the High Court for breach of their constitutional right to privacy.

73

7. ELECTORAL LAW

Some of the most important restrictions on free speech and freedom of information in Ireland and Britain arise not from special legislation but from restrictive measures in ordinary law, and the exercise of executive or judicial authority. One field in which non-emergency legislation restricts freedom of expression is electoral law.

Election deposits

For a political party which contests elections, the most valuable freedom of information is the ability to communicate policies and views directly to the electorate. The law in these islands and elsewhere provides both incentives for electoral communication (such as free postage) and restrictions upon it (such as airtime limits).

Candidates for election to the UK Parliament, to Dáil Eireann (the lower house in the Republic of Ireland) and to the now-suspended parliamentary assemblies of Northern Ireland have to lodge a cash deposit, forfeited if the candidate fails to secure a set proportion of the votes. However, no charge is made for successful candidates, or losers who pass the percentage threshold; the effect of the deposit requirement is that minor, fringe or frivolous candidatures are discouraged.

For a small political party a severe burden is imposed by the requirement to gamble with deposits. The mainstream parties, better able to retain their deposits and less affected by the occasional loss of a few, enjoy mailing privileges and media access while the rest, including those whose commitment to electoral politics is already equivocal, are discouraged from participating.

The amount raised by the forfeiture of deposits is an insignificant proportion of the total cost of running a democratic election, and if society is prepared to pick up the rest of the tab, there is a case for not imposing an entrance fee.

Electoral oaths

On the evidence of the past twenty years, paramilitary violence cannot be defeated by military might; it takes only a few determined individuals to mount a prolonged and costly guerrilla campaign. A more effective way to end the violence might be to convince those who now advocate it to turn to electoral politics as a more ethical and ultimately more effective strategy. The British government has, however, erected a new legal obstacle to electoral participation by requiring candidates for public office within the province to swear an oath renouncing violence.

The Elected Authorities (NI) Act 1988 also disqualified those convicted of criminal offences from council office and stipulated a five-year ban from office for councillors expressing support for terrorism or for a proscribed group.

Junior Minister Richard Needham, introducing the Bill, made it abundantly clear that it was a censorship measure: it would "make it very difficult for the supporters of violence, once elected, to parade their views to the revulsion of councillors and the disgust of the overwhelming majority of the electorate". This tacitly acknowledged that there was a minority of electors whose views would similarly be silenced.

The measure went directly against the advice of the government's own Standing Advisory Commission on Human Rights (SACHR), which said that it was "fundamentally wrong [to] devise artificial means to exclude councillors from local politics; such policies cannot hope to succeed in the long term." Evidence that the government had its own doubts about the measure may be seen in the fact that responsibility for enforcing the oath was left to any member of the public through initiating a private prosecution. For its part, Sinn Féin announced that its candidates would sign the declaration; the smaller Republican Sinn Féin said that its candidates would not.

76

A comparable obstacle, viewed from the standpoint of the Nationalist community in Northern Ireland, is the parliamentary oath of allegiance. Nationalist MPs, and republicans among British MPs, have found it possible to take this oath. On the other hand, the oath question is one of transcendent importance to the Irish Republican movement.

The removal or reformulation of the parliamentary oath may not enable such as Gerry Adams MP to enter the House - there is also the question of whether entry recognises Parliament's right to rule Northern Ireland - but it is certain that he cannot, by his own lights, enter the House under that condition. His right to speak for the people of West Belfast is founded on the same principle as makes the British Prime Minister the representative of Finchley. The oath restricts his right to impart his opinions in the assembly to which he was elected, and so is an obstacle to the cessation of the violence by which his movement currently expresses itself.

Electoral relevance of the broadcasting bans

In an information-based society, public representatives are expected to use the mass media to convey the views of their electorate. It has become one of their essential functions. The Section 31 ban in the Irish Republic, and the 1988 ban in the UK, diminish the effectiveness of dozens of properly elected councillors and one MP by denying them equal access to the broadcast media. This thus constitutes an interference with the rights of electors and elected, and imposes a considerable handicap on the operation of what is, as yet, a legal political party. Despite the relaxation of the UK ban just before elections, unaffected parties have a government-imposed advantage so that elections cannot be said to take place freely and fairly.

Other restrictions on political expression

Civil servants in certain grades or types of employment are prohibited from standing or canvassing in UK elections, holding office in political parties or expressing political views in public speeches or publications. (A Foreign Office civil servant, Patrick Heseldine, was dismissed in July 1989 for sending a letter to *The Guardian* criticising Mrs Thatcher's attitude to the extradition of alleged terrorists.) In the Irish Republic civil servants may not join political parties. Members of the forces are banned from political activity by both states, and there are proposals to restrict the political activity of UK local government employees.

In April 1988 a community worker, Roisin McDonagh, was suspended from her post with Belfast City Council for writing a commissioned article for *The Irish Times* about the "mood of despair" in West Belfast. She was reinstated on condition that she submit future publications for vetting.

A minor restriction on electoral freedom of expression in the Irish Republic is the rule that only parties registered with the Clerk of the Dail may have their names printed on ballot papers.

8. OFFICIAL SECRECY AND ACCESS TO INFORMATION

One of the rights held by article 19 of the Universal Declaration to be a component part of the right to freedom of expression and opinion is the "freedom to... seek [and] receive... information". As the state is one of the principal manufacturers and repositories of data, each citizen should have full access to information held about him or her, or in relation to government policies and activities, with reasonable exceptions to preserve public safety, the proper functions of government, or other genuine public interests. Access is of particular value in relation to potentially prejudicial information about the individual, such as that held by security services, or in relation to activities which may involve the abuse of public trust or funds. Those are, of course, precisely the areas in which access is most difficult.

Official Secrets Acts

Ireland and the UK are not exactly bastions of open government; both states have a long tradition of virtually clandestine operation of Cabinet, ministries and public authorities, with legislation (called, in both states, the Official Secrets Act) defining state secrets in such sweeping terms as to illegitimise almost any disclosure of information gathered or produced by servants of the state. (In practice, of course, efficient government requires frequent breaches of the strict provisions of the law; selective leaks of politically sensitive information, although sometimes punished where they involve civil servants, have since the 1960s been a routine practice of government ministers.)

Under the pressure of insurrectionary violence officials of both states have used these far-reaching secrecy laws to conceal information which many would consider essential to informed public debate. In both states they are mainly used coercively rather than reactively: that is, to encourage public servants to respect confidentiality by requiring them to sign a declaration of secrecy. Actual prosecutions are rare.

In the UK, the replacement in 1989 of the Official Secrets Act 1911 with an even more repressive version is most unlikely to result in a relaxation of secrecy on Irish political and security issues. There are no plans to update the Republic's 1963 Act.

Intelligence agencies

Despite the currency in both the UK and Ireland of the doctrines of parliamentary supremacy, ministerial authority and judicial review, both states have developed a cult of secrecy about the activities of their intelligence services, a cult so pervasive and persuasive that parliaments, ministers and judges have held themselves to have no right to oversee, question or examine the operations of the services or the legitimacy of the information on which they act.

The state has a need to gather information on threats to public order and national security. While it is clear that the collection of certain types of information requires a degree of secrecy, the excessive secrecy in Britain and Ireland as to every aspect of the structure, resources and activities of such agencies results in the abuse both of the powers granted the agencies and of the information gathered.

Intelligence agencies include domestic and international espionage and counter-espionage services, the political (Special) branches of the police forces, signals intelligence bodies and the other military and civilian institutions responsible for collecting and analysing information for the government. The term can also be used more loosely to include covert police or army anti-terrorist, propaganda or disinformation units.

There are three main areas of potential abuse. The agencies may collect more information than is legitimately required, encroaching on the privacy of the individual; they may operate improperly or illegally in the course of their information-gathering activities; and they may make illegal or improper use of the information they possess.

Excessive intelligence gathering

The security forces in Northern Ireland hold a fantastic volume of intelligence information about the general population. As long ago as the mid-1970s Robert Fisk was writing in *The Times* of Army officers in Belfast boasting how they could check with a computer on such details as whether the wallpaper in a given house had been changed since they last searched it. At about the same time the Army was carrying out extensive "census" operations across the province. Police files include not just criminal records but criminal and political intelligence; in both states the police are able to take and retain fingerprints and photographs of unconvicted persons, and in the UK that also applies to DNA typing material.

At the police or military roadblocks which are a constant feature of life in the more troubled areas (approximately 10 million cars are stopped per year), radio links are used to check personal details. One is required under the EPA to give certain information - name, point of departure and destination - but more is frequently asked for, including address and date of birth, and proof of identity is almost always demanded (NI driving licences incorporate a plastic identity card). Declining to answer non- compulsory questions invites hostile treatment, delay and inconvenience, but even criticism of excessive questioning in the government's own annual review of the EPA (undertaken by Lord Balville) has not halted it.

81

Quite apart from the issue of whether the state has a right to hold so much secret and personal data on its citizens, there is a price to be paid for its collection. Civil liberties are breached in the massive effort required to assemble and update this vast database; even the most loyal and peaceable of citizens are subject to constant questioning at roadblocks, analysis of telephone calls and monitoring of movements. The zealous collection of information, while it assists in identifying and investigating suspects, contributes to a general climate of paranoia and resentment in the most affected areas.

Impropriety by intelligence services

Well documented elsewhere, but shortly to be withdrawn by law from the right of information and comment, are abuses of power by the British intelligence services in the 1960s and 1970s, including an apparent conspiracy within MI5 around 1974 to destabilise and overthrow an elected Labour government. It has been alleged that the security services in Northern Ireland were involved in that conspiracy.

Disinformation and psychological warfare operations, consisting largely of feeding false rumours to the media, distorted the public perception of events there to an unknown and probably unknowable extent from the early 1970s onwards.

Possibly the most notorious recent abuse of the concept of official secrecy in relation to the Troubles was the order given to certain RUC officers that they should obstruct an investigation into claims that the force had a "shoot-to-kill" policy in relation to IRA suspects around 1982. The policemen were instructed that to tell the truth would be a breach of the oath they had taken under the Official Secrets Act, and that they were consequently bound to perjure themselves. Vital evidence held by MI5 was destroyed or withheld from the investigators led by John Stalker, who was replaced for what were widely regarded as political reasons. The Stalker revelations, which were not followed by prosecutions, worsened the image of the security forces in the eyes of the Nationalist community.

The Special Branch, as the main intelligence agency in the Republic, has also been accused of abusing its information-gathering powers. During the 1983 campaign against a constitutional amendment prohibiting abortion, Christy Moore and other supporters of a pressure group called Musicians Against the Amendment were allegedly placed under Special Branch observation. [32]

32▷ *Sunday Tribune* 3.9.89

Abuse of secret information

There was considerable concern in September-October 1989 (when this report was prepared) over the apparently unauthorised transfer of intelligence data to Loyalist paramilitaries.

On 25th August a Catholic, Loughlin Maginn, was murdered by a UFF gang working from official intelligence briefing material later shown to a reporter. Although government ministers stated that any such leaks would be punished "with the full severity of the law", and two UDR soldiers have since been charged in connection with the Maginn case, it emerged in early September that a British Army corporal, Cameron Hastie, convicted in connection with a similar transfer of intelligence information to the UVF in 1988, had been retained by his regiment.

On 6th September another intelligence document containing photographs and personal details of nine Republicans was reported missing from a UDR base in Ballykinlar, and it was later revealed that two similar documents had disappeared from Dunmurry RUC station. Other briefing documents and photographic montages of "suspects" turned up from apparently Loyalist sources during the following weeks, bringing the total of compromised "suspects" to around 600, and a major police investigation was announced.

There had been some previous incidents, with documents turning up in a UVF cache in 1987, leading some to conclude that many cases had gone undetected or unreported or that collusion with Loyalist terrorists was widespread and official.

83

Access to information

Neither state has a law guaranteeing full access to personal information held by governments or private bodies. Their Data Protection Acts, which gave individuals the right to inspect computer records on them, specifically excluded most security information.

One consequence is that people who are denied employment in institutions such as the electricity and telecommunications services, and firms who are denied government business, on the grounds of a supposed security risk ("Section 42" cases) have no way of ascertaining or challenging the information used.

Likewise, voluntary bodies can be denied public funding on the basis of secret and unchallengeable "security" information. A celebrated case is that of the Conway Mills community resource centre in West Belfast.

Police accountability

The new Chief Constable of the RUC, Hugh Annesley, said during the leaked files controversy in September 1989 that "a clear facet of honest policing is the disclosure of information which the public have a right to know." [33]

The Police Authority for Northern Ireland - an appointed body to which the RUC is partly answerable - is responsible for the expenditure of £1,000,000 of public money per day, but does not publish an annual report. The names and qualifications of members of the Authority are not disclosed for security reasons, which inevitably detracts from the credibility of the Authority and from the whole notion of police accountability to the public.

84

Official disclosure of information

As well as the withholding of information on legal or security grounds, there are some problems with the official release of non-secret information. One area of concern is inconsistency of data on the operation of the emergency legislation (numbers arrested or questioned under the PTA, EPA and so on). Statistics on house searches by the security forces relate the number of searches to the volume of illegal items, for example bullets or explosives, which have been found; the government has never reported the ratio of unsuccessful searches - where homes may be virtually

33>   *The Guardian* 22.9.89

destroyed, to no effect other than antagonising the residents - to successful searches, i.e. where something is found. Statistics have recently been revised to show that only 263 houses were entered in the first half of 1988 rather than 1,752 as previously stated.

Many parliamentary questions on the Troubles are replied to incompletely or not at all, either because of a policy of not commenting on security issues or because of the supposedly inordinate cost of compiling the information. Another manoeuvre, as used in response to an April 1988 question on RUC conduct, is to give written answers to avoid follow-up questioning.

It is often difficult to obtain reliable information from official sources on matters of public interest. The NI *Yearbook*, which gave a wide range of socio-economic and political data, is no longer published. Different branches of the government issue conflicting statistics on, for example, the sentencing of prisoners, or complaints against the RUC, due perhaps to inefficiency but with the effect of muddying the waters for outside investigators.

The non-cooperation of a public body may result in the censorship of the media. In 1977 the RUC refused to give an interview for a Thames TV *This Week* programme on maltreatment of detainees. The IBA insisted that the programme could not go ahead without a "balancing" contribution from the RUC, and Thames had eventually to accept a five-minute RUC statement to camera with no opportunity to question the speaker.

85

On the positive side, it should be noted that in September 1989 the British Army decided for the first time to release (to *The Guardian* newspaper) politically sensitive statistics on the number (239) of serious criminal convictions of soldiers serving in Northern Ireland in the previous two years. The Army refused to allow an interview or give figures for unsuccessful prosecutions or complaints not prosecuted.

Government archives

In both states, government documents are filed away for 30, 50 or more years according to the sensitivity of the information and whether publication would breach a confidence. Researchers are liable to find that officials have weeded out vital papers before storing or releasing the file; alternatively, the file or parts of it may be reclassified and consigned to darkness for another 20 years or more.

Some documents relating to British rule in Ireland up to 1921 are regarded as so secret that their contents may not be known until 100 years after the events to which they relate. The problem is not new; it has been mentioned by many historians of modern Ireland.

It may never be known how much Stormont material has been, or will be, weeded before public access is permitted. A leading librarian in the province has complained specifically about the removal of political material from files in the NI Public Records Office. The RUC has also withheld documents seized in raids when there is no longer any possible security value, for example the minutes of unofficial camp council meetings in Long Kesh prison during the early 1970s.

Secrecy and censorship in prisons

The NI prison population is, at about 1,700 sentenced prisoners, more than one per thousand of the general populace. A high proportion are imprisoned for what may be regarded as political offences. There are in addition a considerable number imprisoned or remanded in Britain or in the Republic for offences connected with the Troubles.

To what extent do, or should, prisoners have civil rights? By definition they have lost the right to liberty, with the secondary freedoms dependent on that - freedom of movement, a normal family life and so on. But it does not follow that their rights in respect of the free flow of information are, or should be, withdrawn by the prison sentence, or transformed into discretionary privileges. A House of Lords ruling in 1983 said that a prisoner "retains all rights which are not taken away expressly or by implication", but in practice the prison system has discretion to withdraw what are regarded outside prison as rights.

A fundamental aspect of the freedom of expression is the right to participate in political discussion. Prisoners have no right to vote in either state, and after the election and death of Bobby Sands MP in 1981 they were deprived of the right to stand for election in the UK. Thus their ability to participate in national politics is severely restricted. If there is a genuine intention to convert paramilitaries into law-abiding citizens, it would be logical to integrate them as far as possible in the institutions and processes of civil society by restoring the vote, lifting restrictions on educational activities, and permitting and even encouraging prisoners to join parties and engage in political debate.

In both states, prisoners normally have no access to telephones and there is official censorship of the incoming and outgoing correspondence. In addition a record is kept in NI prisons of those with whom a prisoner exchanges letters, and this data is given to Life Sentence Review Boards. Prisoners have been denied the right to correspond in the Irish language, and Irish-language bibles were confiscated in November 1987.

Prisoners are not normally allowed to give television or radio interviews, although one might have thought that society, particularly in Northern Ireland, could only gain from a heightened awareness of prison life and the opportunity to observe the criminal personality. (During the 1980-81 hunger strikes, there was a small concession: one TV company was allowed to put one question to one hunger striker.) Press interviews are also severely restricted; the normal practice has been to require journalists visiting prisoners to sign a form promising not to publish anything about the visit. Restrictions on the receipt of publications by prisoners have in theory been lifted after European Court action, but some NI prisoners - for example in the new Maghaberry prison - report continued difficulty and delay in obtaining books and journals.

The origins of this restriction of communication are obscure - certainly it has been the rule in both British and Irish prisons for at least a century. There is no public outcry and most prisoners take censorship for granted; but it is an intrusion into the privacy of the prisoners and those who wish to correspond with them, and one which the European Court has condemned.

With the presumed concern of the prison authorities to provide a humane and, if possible, rehabilitative regime, this is an area where reform could be considered. No amount of communication into or out of a well-run prison should imperil security; the abolition of censorship would have the compensatory benefits of creating a less oppressive relationship with the staff and enhancing constructive contact between the prisoner and his family and friends.

Prisoners serving life or indeterminate sentences in Northern Ireland (27 per cent of the total, against 6 per cent in Britain) are considered by the Life Sentence Review Board, which determines when a prisoner may be released or after how many years his case should next be reviewed. The criteria used are secret, so that prisoners do not actually know what they may do to increase their chances of release; decisions are arrived at in secret; neither the prisoner nor his legal representative may attend; the prisoner is not allowed legal aid or assistance; he has no access to, or right to challenge, the statements made about him and other information on which the decision is based; the reasons for an unfavourable decision are not formally advised to the prisoner, although as a very recent concession a brief oral account may be given.

In the Republic the position is, if anything, worse in that there is no Review Board and no information is given to prisoners by the Department of Justice on its internal review procedures.

Book censorship

A threat to the availability of information on the administration of Northern Ireland is the present British government's obsessional pursuit of some isolated instances of unauthorised disclosures in books by former public servants, where no damage to national security is involved or where greater damage could conceivably result from non-disclosure.

The celebrated late 1980s cases of the *Spycatcher* book and another autobiography, *One Girl's War* by former MI5 operative Joan Miller, are of special interest in the Irish context. The indifference of the Republic's courts to the purported lifelong duty of confidentiality led to the situation whereby books banned in the North were sold openly, since there was no way of stopping their importation across the border.

Disclosures of improper activity by security agencies in Northern Ireland appear in Paul Foot's book about a former military intelligence operative (*Who Framed Colin Wallace?*, Macmillan, London, 1989), and in a similar but autobiographical account from Frank Holroyd. Other books on MI5 and Northern Ireland are in preparation.

Another case in which the book industry has been affected by what might be seen as a censorship measure in Northern Ireland was the November 1988 arrest and 24-hour detention under the Prevention of Terrorism Act of Peter Clifford of Pathfinder Press. He had just visited a customer in the Maze prison and said that his interrogation focused on the sales and plans of his company.

Inquests and public inquiries

If the purpose of an inquest into a death is to establish information, then anything which delays, prevents or interferes with it constitutes an impediment to freedom of information. In Northern Ireland there are a large number of adjourned or still unopened inquests on victims of the Troubles; some of the cases date back to 1982 and are still the focus of heated political debate.

The first inquest into the six 1982 Stalker case killings by the RUC opened only in November 1988 (after a coroner resigned over irregularities in police files). An inquest on three men shot by the Army in 1985 took place in 1987, with numerous procedural errors. The inquest on Aidan McAnespie, killed by an Army bullet in February 1988, was not opened until November 1988 and was then postponed indefinitely.

Another obstacle to the pursuit of truth at inquests arises from the use of Public Interest Immunity Certificates, which can prevent the disclosure of evidence. This procedure was used in the inquest held in Gibraltar into the killing there of three IRA personnel in 1988. Those killings have been the subject of several demands for a public or judicial inquiry. Demands for public inquiries into other controversies arising from the Troubles have frequently been ignored by the authorities.

9. FIGHTING CENSORSHIP

Censorship of political information and opinion is more than an injury to a basic civil right: it is an insult to the intelligence of the people. It implies that there are those who are qualified to judge what we may and may not be permitted to see - what is bland enough to be safe, and what is a little too dangerous or persuasive to risk exposure to the masses. The advocates of censorship often regard themselves as among an intellectual elite which is immune from the effects of propaganda, but which has a duty to protect the ordinary people: witness the arguments put forward in favour of the 1988 UK broadcasting ban.

Following the announcement of the ban in the Commons Unionist MP Ken Maginnis said that it was "aimed at protecting, not the intelligent viewer, but young people who can be influenced by the likes of Gerry Adams... on television". Surprisingly, the implication that news and current affairs broadcasting - the main affected areas - ought to be circumscribed to what is incapable of affecting the stupid or the immature went unchallenged in the House. *The Times* picked up Mr Maginnis's line: "the unthinking viewer can be all too easily swayed".

Opposition within the media

In choosing their profession broadcasters and journalists have assumed a duty to the public, an obligation which transcends considerations of policy and personal advancement. Not only must they resist self-censorship in their own work and in their media; with a little imagination and effort they can use their positions to expose, challenge and ridicule imposed censorship. Some of the ways in which they can do, and occasionally have done, are discussed in Chapter 5 (Self-censorship). With a few exceptions, they have chosen the more comfortable path of acquiescence.

There have always been some who are willing to take risks and make sacrifices to register their opposition. During the 1970's, leading investigative BBC reporters, Peter Taylor, Jonathan Dimbleby and Keith Kyle, expressed alarm in articles in the *Listener* over neglect of the Northern Ireland question and growing censorship pressures. Most censorship decisions follow internal discussion in the media organisation, authority, institution or government body concerned, and there are many who have defended free speech in such discussions, or who have made representations or protests to their managements. If resistance is confined to such discreet and internal advocacy, however, it is almost inevitable that the resisters will be worn down over time: no-one wants to stand out in what Irish broadcaster Prionsias Mac Aonghusa describes as "a censorship culture" as the one awkward individual who champions every unpopular cause. It is preferable by far that the protest should be public, since it is the public whose rights are infringed by censorship and it is public pressure which can bring change.

Resistance can take many forms. In 1971, Granada TV carried on making a *World in Action* programme, "South of the Border", after the ITA had banned it; the ITA looked at the finished product and confirmed the ban. In 1979 the BBC tested the perception that the 1974 PTA prevented interviews with terrorists by broadcasting one with an INLA spokesman; the government backed down from a threat to prosecute and the five-year de facto ban was ended. In 1982 the BBC re-broadcast a censored documentary, *Children in Crossfire* (1974), but other censored or criticised programmes have been denied repeats.

Sometimes broadcasters have attempted to insert "health warnings" in censored films (but in the 1976 and 1977 showings of a BBC Scotland documentary, the producers' statement was deliberately omitted) or they have left the screens blank to demonstrate the position and duration of cuts. On one notable occasion a media union forced the issue; the ACTT shop in Thames simply refused to broadcast a substitute for a banned Thames documentary on RUC ill-treatment of detainees in 1978, and screens remained blank. RTE journalists threatened to suspend coverage of the 1983

Westminster elections in those NI constituencies where Sinn Fééin candidates could not be interviewed, but a subsequent meeting backed down. In 1985, journalists throughout UK broadcasting staged a 24-hour strike to protest at government interference in the *Real Lives* case. Strikes were contemplated soon after the 1988 ban, but were called off; the next day Mrs Thatcher told a Polish audience how important "openness and freedom of speech" was to modern societies.

Those involved in making programmes have issued statements or open letters denouncing censorship (Robert Holles, *The Vanishing Army* BBC, 1979, and members of the *Open Door* selection panel, BBC, 1982). Others have asked that their names be removed from the credits of programmes which have been interfered with: writer Shane Connaughton in 1977 (*Eighteen Months to Balcombe Street*, LWT), and writer Caryl Churchill and director Roland Joffe in 1978 (*Play for Today*, BBC). Where the issue is sufficiently important, some have resigned (Colin Thomas, BBC director; 1978, the BBC Controller NI, 1985, persuaded to withdraw) or have had themselves dismissed (Roger Bolton, BBC editor; 1979, won reinstatement).

A novel way of circumventing the ban imposed by one authority is to show the material, or parts of it, on another network. BBC's *Nationwide* showed extracts of the banned Thames documentary on torture in 1978; ATV's *Tiswas* showed a pop video on Belfast banned by the BBC in 1981. Some broadcasters have assisted legal challenges to censorship measures. Other useful ways of highlighting censorship are to publish information or make programmes about it (BBC2 16th November 1988; BBC1 9th January 1989; but such programmes can themselves be censored, as in the 1979 *Spotlight* case), to give public showings to affected programmes (the banned *Mother Ireland* film from Derry, now distributed on video), or to award prizes (*Creggan*, 1980, won two major awards but even the censored version has been denied a repeat showing). Secrecy in the "Section 42" employment cases (see Chapter 8) has also been criticised in a BBC programme, *Taking Liberties*.

Broadcasting other than under the auspices of the IBA or the BBC is not covered by the 1988 UK ban, so UKC Radio, a

93

student-run station at the University of Kent at Canterbury, decided to broadcast a speech made there by a Sinn Féin member in January 1989. The general secretary of the Students' Union subsequently received a death threat.

Legal challenges to the UK broadcasting ban

Within weeks of the UK ban the NUJ announced that it was to mount a legal challenge to it and to Section 31 in Ireland. ARTICLE 19 has played a co-ordinating role in the litigation. The broadcasting authorities declined to join the case.

In May 1989 the UK case opened in the High Court.[34] Seven broadcast journalists sought judicial review, making several points; the ban was unnecessary in view of the trifling amount of coverage given in the past and the anti-terrorist tenor and effect of such coverage; it was difficult to apply; it removed editorial control from broadcasters to the government; it prevented the public being fully and impartially informed; and it forced broadcasters to police themselves as to whether views and utterances were broadcastable. The judgment, however, held that the Home Secretary was acting within the very wide powers given him by the Statute, Licence and Agreement, making political judgements within his discretion and competence and in accordance with the exceptions specified in article 10 of the European Convention; the ban might have been disproportionate to the mischief supposedly prevented or the benefit obtained, but the powers of judicial review did not extend to such instances.

The case will be argued before the Court of Appeal in November; thereafter if unsucceful the applicants intend to take it to the European Commission of Human Rights.

The National Council for Civil Liberties (Liberty/NCCL) issued proceedings in early 1989 on behalf of a Brighton Labour councillor, Richard Stanton, whose speech at a local meeting on Northern Ireland had been censored by television and radio

94

34> <u>Regina v Secretary of State for the Home Dept.</u>, ex parte Brind & others, in the High Court, Queen's Bench Division

stations. The case had to be abandoned in May when Mr Stanton was refused legal aid. Another case brought in the High Court in Belfast by Sinn Féin councillor Mitchell McLaughlin foundered when he was also refused legal aid in June 1989. Both applicants had hoped to contest the ban up to the European Court.

The interesting possibility exists that the ban, precisely because it is aimed at NI organisations, has no legal effect in the province, at least as it affects the BBC. The Northern Ireland Constitution Act 1973 prohibits the government from discriminating on political grounds unless acting under an Act of Parliament; the BBC ban was made under a Licence and Agreement, not an Act, and would thus appear to be open to challenge and injunction in the NI courts (depending on an interpretation of the 1949 Act under which the Licence was issued).

Legal challenge to Section 31 and the Irish Broadcasting Ban

In August 1989 the NUJ and the Federated Workers' Union of Ireland with the assistance of ARTICLE 19 launched a challenge to the Irish broadcasting ban with the European Commission of Human Rights. The applicants cite three articles of the European Convention: those governing freedom of expression, discrimination and the right to effective remedies. They also refer to a Protocol of the Convention concerning freedom of expression in connection with elections. The challenge relies partly on affidavits from journalists and others affected by the ban and importantly includes affidavits from the management of RTE; the Director General, Vincent Finn, the Director of Radio News, Michael Goode, Wesley Boyd, Director of Television and the Comtroller of TV and Radio, Mr Bob Collins. No decision is expected before late 1990.

95

Campaigning activity

Several organisations have decided, or been created, to combat censorship and to promote freedom of information within and in relation to Northern Ireland. The media unions, civil liberties groups, the Campaign for Free Speech on Ireland, Information on Ireland, the Committee on the Administration of Justice, the Repeal Section 31 Committee, Media Watch, the Campaign for Press and Broadcasting Freedom (CPBF) have all campaigned on Irish information rights in recent years. ARTICLE 19 has campaigned on these issues and others in Ireland and Britain from the standpoint of the international standards on freedom of information and freedom of expression. This report isa further contribution. There are many other local, national and international organisations which address one or more of the issues identified in this report from a political, religious or humanitarian perspective.

Liberty/NCCL has been active on a number of secrecy issues related to the Troubles. In 1988 it was represented in a panel which reported on the secret political vetting of community groups seeking public funding.[35] With the New York-based International League for Human Rights it has co- published a book on the Gibraltar killings[36] which inter alia supports the calls for a new, full and public inquiry into the events.

A "Petition Against the Ban" was organised in July- August 1989 by the CPBF, and secured the support of many MPs, trade union leaders, lawyers, entertainers, writers and other prominent personalities. The petition was presented to 10 Downing Street on 19th October, the first anniversary of the ban.

The West Belfast newspaper *Andersonstown News* organised an anti-censorship conference in December 1988, and numerous local gatherings across Britain and Ireland have discussed the issues and watched censored TV films such as *Mother Ireland*. Sinn Féin has made its own "news videos".

96

35> details from Community Groups Against Vetting, Conway Mill, Conway Street, Belfast

36> *The Gibraltar Report*, Hilary Kitchen, 1989

10. CONCLUSIONS

The Troubles in Northern Ireland have imposed great suffering on the people of that province, and to a lesser degree on those of Britain and the Irish state. They have been accompanied by official and unofficial encroachment on civil and political rights, including many of the rights contained within or dependent on the freedom of information. Since much of this activity has been explained and defended in terms of the stated need to give priority to the suppression of terrorism, it raises two fundamental concerns: does it work, and is it right?

Does it work?

In what ways, and to what degree, have the various restrictive measures and practices described above, and the general lack of openness and accessibility of information, hampered the search for a permanent and peaceful solution to the complex problems of communal relationships within and between the islands of Ireland and Britain?

That is, perhaps, an imponderable, even in relation to the events of the past twenty years. The civil rights movement of the late 1960s might not have been fuelled by such resentment had not the Stormont government sought for 45 years to marginalise and disable minority political expression by a combination of gerrymandering and coercion. The backlash from the majority community might have been less unthinkingly destructive had it not become accustomed to the notion that there was no such thing as a right to peaceful protest - that dissent, in fact, equalled subversion. And if the combination of Catholic/Nationalist frustration and Protestant/Unionist intransigence had been able to find open and honest expression in representative institutions, and if the lack of informed interest on the part of media and national parliaments had not prevented the raising of the issues before

97

the wider British and Irish public, the situation might not have degenerated so rapidly and seemingly irrevocably into irrational and self-perpetuating brutality.

It requires a longer historical perspective, and more information, than is now available to analyse the strategic thinking behind the response of the provincial, British and Irish authorities to the eruption of street protest and violence. The first thought of any government threatened with internal revolt has always been to first extinguish the flames, and then seek causes and preventative measures. If that was the reasoning of the British and Northern Irish authorities, as successive memoirs and revelations appear to confirm, then it has to be pointed out that the fires are still burning twenty years on.

Something more than, something other than counter-insurgency techniques, however sophisticated, is needed. Nor will silencing or ignoring dissent encourage it to go away; the effects are quite the opposite. Censorship, and its inevitable companion, self-censorship, oblige those whose views are suppressed to find alternative means of access to the headlines. The appearance of indifference to the root causes of the conflict, as opposed to the containment of the resulting violence, is one of the most powerful incentives for the disaffected to turn to revolutionary rather than persuasive approaches.

98

There is no published evidence whatever that, to take one of the censorship measures, the 1988 UK broadcasting ban has had the predicted effect of diminishing support for the 11 listed organisations. Some very crude potential indicators are available, such as the Sinn Féin vote - which in the 1989 local government elections held to within 0.7 per cent of the previous level, although some seats were lost - and the number of deaths, which in the year after the ban was lower than in the year before it (although murders by Loyalist gangs affected by the ban remained at the same level). Not even the staunchest defenders of the ban have publicly suggested to date that the overall decline in deaths (roughly, from 100 to 75) was wholly, or even significantly, attributable to it; as in the maintenance of the SF vote, all sorts of other factors could be cited. Just as the decline in deaths might have been greater without the ban, so might the ban have boosted the SF vote; it is simply impossible to say. And if it is impossible to measure the impact of the ban, how can it be viewed as a temporary measure - on what basis will the government decide to renew or end it?

Is it right?

The question of whether repression of information rights is ever justified may be approached from at least three perspectives. The first sees certain human rights including information rights as inalienable, and demands that even under duress a democratic society live and defend itself by the rules and mores appropriate to more settled times. Many in Ireland and Britain take that uncompromising stance and need no persuasion from ARTICLE 19.

The second view is that the enjoyment or curtailment of rights is conditional on the stability or otherwise of a particular society at any given moment. Those who hold that view would say that there are higher-value rights, such as the right to life, and lower-value rights, such as freedom of expression, and that the lower-value rights of some or all may be suspended where necessary or expedient in combatting a threat to the enjoyment of the more fundamental rights. The key idea is *suspension*, for it is assumed that the deprivation of rights is only *temporary*, until such time as the threat has receded or the suspension has proven to have a nil or negative effect. Thus one ultimately returns to the first question of whether the repression works.

99

The third view imputes a degree of reciprocity to the existence or otherwise of a right: those who allow others to enjoy their rights should enjoy equal rights, but those who infringe the rights of others should lose the protection of some of their own rights. It is, of course, the basis of criminal law that a crime, which is invariably an infringement of rights, justifies the punishment of the perpetrator, usually by deprivation of liberty or property, but it does not follow that the concept has a more general application, as in saying that a section of the population which opposes an incumbent government thereby loses entitlement to the protection of the state, which in a democracy exists to serve the whole people.

The more limited argument that those who seek the abolition of the state should not be permitted to use state-controlled broadcasting systems to advocate their position (the basis of the Irish Government's ban) is equally unattractive, for it implies that the state's first duty in its role as public trustee is to promote its own interests as defined by the incumbent government, and this has immediately apparent dangers if extended to the duties and functions of the state in any other area.

It is, in essence, an untenable position in a democratic society to justify depriving individual citizens of a liberty not because of any criminal act on their part but because the state does not like the way they think. (To suggest that the deprivation is not individual, but collective, as for example in restricting only those who claim to be speaking on behalf of an organisation, is surely specious; if the state recognises a right to free association, as both the Irish and UK authorities do in the case of Sinn Féin and the UDA, no- one can justly be penalised for exercising of that right.)

Defending the right of dissident political groupings to have their opinions aired and challenged by the broadcasting media on the same basis and within the same limitations as those applied to mainstream parties does not imply any sympathy either for the particular standpoint of the dissidents or for the tactics which they adopt. Indeed, affording such opportunity provides the means to communicate the majority's abhorrence of such tactics and standpoints.

100

The way forward

The only way forward in Northern Ireland is to turn people away from violence and towards political debate. Censorship undoubtedly impedes this process. Those who are most passionately opposed to the violence of Ireland's paramilitary groups, and who are most serious about ending that violence, must think not of how best to defeat them militarily - the evidence so far is that that simply cannot be done - but rather of how to defeat them through political debate with their supporters, and, simultaneously, how to persuade the individuals who are now killing people regardless of laws, ethics and personal consequences to stop doing so.

That means openly examining, discussing, analysing and directly addressing the political stances and the tactical approaches taken by such groups and their public apologists, and persuading those who now support such groups that there is either a better fundamental goal or a more effective, and ethical, means of achieving or defeating the purpose on which they are currently focused. If the British and Irish governments are serious in presenting themselves as arbiters in, rather than parties to, the Northern strife, then they must encourage debate and dialogue.

That means allowing those who speak for all groups, but *especially* those who now communicate through violence, to put their case on television, on the radio and in the print media, and allowing their arguments to stand or fall on their merits, in open interplay with the views advanced by the many opposing and competing political forces.

Responsible journalism can operate in ways other than the anti-journalism of the gagging laws. It can actually work by allowing journalists more leeway to express their own views, rather than heaping specific bans on top of the already limiting ethos of "impartial" broadcasting. When Enniskillen happened - and there will be more Enniskillens - there was no-one to whom the broadcast media, as the interlocutors of civil society with the men of violence, could put the simple question: "How can you possibly justify this?" There was no-one whose blustering apology could be exhibited, confronted and countered. Popular abhorrence of terroristic violence naturally extends into the media professions, but letting its proponents be heard and letting journalists editorialise on behalf of the majority are a better defence than pretending that such people do not exist.

Will the new broadcasting regime in the 1990s - new television channels and authorities, new national and local radio stations - have any effect on freedom of information issues in relation to the Irish troubles? Too early to say, perhaps; it is more than likely that new operators will be subjected to the same, or even stricter, controls as the existing channels, and the downward pressure on journalistic standards which some foresee as a likely consequence of greater competition may actually reduce the amount or standard of coverage.

In the meantime, there is an urgent need for all those who value the rights of the individual - rights which are violated not only be terrorism but by unacceptable government action - to analyse, understand and oppose censorship and secrecy.

The protection of freedom of information and freedom of expression in both societies needs more than a new approach to these freedoms in the context of Northern Ireland. It requires a new approach to thee rights in British and Irish society as a whole. A democratic society is an open society. It should not accept that the murky world of secrecy, security agencies and the powers that they deploy are beyond its scrutiny. To the contrary, all information, including information on the functions and activities of all security services, should be accessible to the public except where it can be clearly demonstrated to independent judicial authority that disclosure will compromise the privacy of the individual or the enforcement of the law. The use and abuse of national security and anti-terrorism justifications for censorship and secreecy on both sides of the Irish border underlines the need for freedom of information laws in both countries. The Parliaments of both states should as an initial step debate censorship and secrecy over Northern Ireland as outlined in this report, with a view to establishing the full accountability of all security agencies through clear, visible and defensible laws.

The broadcasting bans in both countries should be withdrawn, but beyond that there is a need for new legal guarantees of the editorial independence of the broadcaster. It is for the programme maker and the journalist to decide, subject to the ordinary law, who may be interviewed on television or radio. It is not the role of government to determine the political content of broadcasting or of any other media. ARTICLE 19 believes that such interference cannot be justified under the international standards for the protection of freedom of expression and freedom of the media, standards which both governments are bound to uphold.

11. BIBLIOGRAPHY AND ABBREVIATIONS

Some of the literature and organisations listed below and concerned with freedom of information issues in the context of the Irish Troubles take a partisan stance with which ARTICLE 19 does not associate itself. Particular thanks are due to the Committee on the Administration of Justice; David Millar of the Glasgow Media Group; Liz Curtis; Mike Jempson, Mike Mullan and Liam Clarke.

Further reading

☐ The British Media and Ireland - Truth: the first casualty. Campaign for Free Speech on Ireland, London, n.d. 1979

☐ Censoring "the Troubles": an Irish solution to an Irish problem. International Federation of Journalists, Brussels, 1987

☐ Civil Liberty, newsletter of the National Council for Civil Liberties, London

☐ Free Press, journal of the Campaign for Press and Broadcasting Freedom, London

☐ Freedom of information: the law, the practice and the ideal. P.J. Birkinshaw, Weidenfeld & Nicolson, London, 1988

☐ The Hurd Broadcasting Ban: a synopsis of press coverage. Mike Jempson, NUJ/CPBF, London, 1988

☐ Ireland: the Censored Subject, Danny Morrison, Sinn Féin, Belfast, 1989

☐ Ireland: the Propaganda War. Liz Curtis, Pluto Press, London, 1984

103

☐ Just News, journal of the Committee on the Administration of Justice, Belfast

☐ Justice under Fire. Anthony Jennings (ed.), Pluto Press, London, 1988

☐ Life Sentence and SOSP Prisoners in Northern Ireland. CAJ, Belfast, 1988

☐ Media law: the rights of journalists, broadcasters and publishers. G. Robertson & A.G.L. Nicolson, Sage Publications, London, 1984

☐ The Most Contrary Region: the BBC in Northern Ireland 1924- 1984. Rex Cathcart, Blackstaff, Belfast, 1984

☐ Official secrets: the use and abuse of the Act. D. Hooper, Secker & Warburg, London, 1987

☐ Police Accountability in Northern Ireland. CAJ, Belfast, 1988

☐ Political violence and the law in Ireland. G. Hogan & C. Walker, Manchester University Press, 1989

☐ Regina v Secretary of State for the Home Department. ex parte Brind and others (unrevised judgement, on the broadcasting ban, ref. CO/1756/88), in the High Court, Queen's Bench Division, Crown Office, London, 1988

☐ Stranger on the Line: the secret history of phone tapping. P. Fitzgerald & M. Leopold, The Bodley Head, London, 1987

☐ The Windlesham-Rampton Report on Death on the Rock. Faber & Faber, London, 1989

104

Contacts - Addresses

The following organisations and institutions document and/or campaign on many of the issues described in this report.

☐ Campaign for Press and Broadcasting Freedom

9 Poland St, London W1V 3DG; (01) 437 2795; formed 1979 to work for fair and accurate reporting

☐ Committee on the Administration of Justice

45-47 Donegall Street, Belfast BT9 6GE; (0232) 232394; civil liberties pressure group

☐ Committee to Protect Journalists

16 West 42nd Street, 3rd Floor, New York, NY 10017; (212) 983-5355. Investigates and protests violations of press freedom around the world.

☐ Derry Film & Video Collective

1 Westend Park, Derry; (0504) 260326; makers of the *Mother Ireland* feature banned from Channel 4

☐ Index on Censorship

39c Highbury Place, London N5 1QP; (01) 359 0161; documents censorship and publishes affected material in magazine of the same name.

☐ Information on Ireland

PO Box 958, London W14 0JF; (01) 602 4195; publishes information about Ireland additional to that given by the national media

☐ International Federation of Journalists

International Press Centre, Bvd Charlemagne, Bte 8, B-1041 Brussels, Belgium; (2) 238 0951; federation of media trade unions

☐ International Journalism Institute

Ruzova 7, 11000 Prague 1, Czechoslovakia. Publisher of regular bulletins on press freedom.

☐ Irish Council for Civil Liberties

4 Nassau Street, Dublin 2. Civil Rights pressure group.

☐ Irish Information Partnership

11 Campion Road, London SW15; (01) 789 5233; compiles and publishes statistical information and analysis on the Troubles

☐ Liberty/National Council for Civil Liberties

21 Tabard Street, London SE1 4LA; (01) 403 3888; the main civil rights pressure group in Britain

☐ **Media Watch**

c/o Resource Publications, PO Box 1494, Dublin 1; modelled on the British CPBF (see above)

☐ **National Union of Journalists**

Acorn House, 314 Gray's Inn Road, London WC1X 8DP; (01) 278 7916; or 8th Floor, Liberty Hall, Dublin 1; (01) 748694; the main union for print and broadcast journalists in Britain and Ireland

☐ **Repeal Section 31 Committee**

c/o USI, 16 North Great George Street, Dublin 1; campaigns for abolition of the Republic's broadcasting ban

☐ **Standing Advisory Commission on Human Rights**

55 Royal Avenue, Belfast BT1 1TA, Tel. (0232) 243987; government- appointed "watchdog" on human rights abuses in Northern Ireland

Author information

This report was initially drafted in September 1989 by Ciarán Ó Maoláin, a freelance journalist based in Northern Ireland. ARTICLE 19 staff modified, completed and edited the text. ARTICLE 19 wishes to thank all the organisations and individuals who contributed information for this report.

Special thanks are due to Trog for kindlly donating his cartoon which illustrates the cover.

Abbreviations

☐ **BBC**   British Broadcasting Coorporation

☐ **CAJ**   Committee on the Administration of Justice

☐ **Cllr**   Councillor

☐ **DUP**   Democratic Unionist Party

☐ **EC**   European Community

- [ ] **EPA**   Emergency Provisions Act
- [ ] **GCHQ**   Government Communications Headquarters
- [ ] **IBA**   Independent Broadcasting Authority
- [ ] **INLA**   Irish National Liberation Army
- [ ] **IRA**   Irish Republican Army
- [ ] **ITA**   Independent Television Authority
- [ ] **ITN**   Independent Television News
- [ ] **ITV**   Independent Television
- [ ] **MEP**   Member of the European Parliament
- [ ] **MI5**   UK domestic security agency
- [ ] **MI6**   UK foreign intelligence agency
- [ ] **MP**   Member of Parliament
- [ ] **NCCL**   Liberty/National Council for Civil Liberties
- [ ] **NI**   Northern Ireland
- [ ] **OASA**   Offences against the State Act
- [ ] **PACE**   Police and Criminal Evidence (Act or Order)
- [ ] **PPB**   Party Political Broadcast
- [ ] **PTA**   Prevention of Terrorism Act
- [ ] **RTE**   Radio Telefis Eireann
- [ ] **RUC**   Royal Ulster Constabulary
- [ ] **SACHR** Standing Advisory Commission on Human Rights
- [ ] **SDLP**   Social Democratic and Labour Party
- [ ] **SDP**   Social Democratic Party
- [ ] **SF**   Sinn Féin
- [ ] **SLD**   Social and Liberal Democrats
- [ ] **TD**   Teachta Dala (member of Irish parliament)
- [ ] **UDA**   Ulster Defence Association
- [ ] **UDR**   Ulster Defence Regiment
- [ ] **UFF**   Ulster Freedom Fighters
- [ ] **UTV**   Ulster Television

☐ **UUP**   Ulster Unionist Party
☐ **UVF**   Ulster Volunteer Force

RECENT PUBLICATIONS FROM ARTICLE 19

"The ARTICLE 19 World Report 1988: Information, Freedom and Censorship"

ARTICLE 19. Published by Times Books, a division of Random House, New York, 1988 and Random House, Canada 1988. ISBN: 0-8129-1801-0. Price U.S.A. $ 22.00 and Longman Group UK Limited, London 1988. ISBN 0-582-02624-5. Price U.K. £ 14.95.

"Journalism Under Occupation: Israel's Regulation of the Palestinian Press"

ARTICLE 19 and The Committee to Protect Journalists, New York, October 1988. ISBN 0-938 579-45-2. Price U.K. £ 4.95 or U.S.A. $8 inc. p&p.

In the Shadow of Buendia. The Mass Media and Censorship in Mexico.

ARTICLE 19. London. July 1989. ISBN 1-870798-26-0 Price U.K. £ 4.95 or U.S.A. $ 8.00 inc. p&p.

109

The Year of the Lie. Censorship and Disinformation in the People's Republic of China 1989

ARTICLE 19. London. September 1989. ISBN 1-870798-31-7. Price U.K..£3.50 inc. p&p.

ARTICLE 19 Commentaries on Freedom of Information and Expression.

Special reports by ARTICLE 19 on the protection of freedom of information and expression in a variety of countries. The series to date includes reports on:

Australia, Barbados, Belgium, Central African Republic, Colombia, Congo, Ecuador, France, Guinea, Hong Kong, Iraq, Japan, Mexico, New Zealand, Norway, Poland, Philippines, Romania, Rwanda, Senegal, Togo, Trinidad and Tobago, Tunisia, Uruguay, Zambia and Zaire.

The complete series provides a unique collection of authentic documents and in-depth analysis combined with a list of sources and reference materials. Commentaries are available separately or in the form of a yearly subscription

SUBSCRIPTION DETAILS

To subscribe to the ARTICLE 19 series on freedom of information and expression in the world (approx. 12 reports per year) the yearly rate is:
£20 ($35) per year for individuals. £30 ($50) per year for institutions.
Please add for post and packaging: Europe: £5 ($8.50).- Elsewhere: £5 ($8.50) for surface mail or £15 ($25) for airmail.

The price of a single copy:
£2.50 ($4) per copy (individuals). £5.00 ($8.50) per copy (institutions). Please add for post and packaging Europe £0.50.($0.85) Elsewhere £1.30 ($2.00) airmail or £0.50 ($0.85) surface mail.